ALSO BY JACQUELINE WELD

Peggy: The Wayward Guggenheim

RARA AVIS

RARA

JACQUELINE WELD

AVIS

BOOKS & CO.

NEW YORK

Jacqueline Weld

RARA AVIS
© 1998 JACQUELINE BOGRAD WELD

LIBRARY OF CONGRESS
CATALOG CARD NUMBER: 98-70430
ISBN: 1-885983-29-8

CATALOGING-IN-PUBLICATION DATA
WELD, JACQUELINE BOGRAD.
RARA AVIS / JACQUELINE BOGRAD WELD. — 1ST ED.
P.   CM.
1. PARROTS — FICTION.   2. TROPICS — FICTION.
3. SOUTH AMERICA — FICTION.   4. POLITICAL
CRIMES AND OFFENSES — SOUTH
AMERICA — FICTION.   I. TITLE.
PS3573.E4554R37   1998   813'.54
QBI98-920

DESIGN AND COMPOSITION BY
WILSTED & TAYLOR PUBLISHING SERVICES

PRINTED IN THE U.S.A.

PUBLISHED AND DISTRIBUTED
IN COOPERATION WITH
TURTLE POINT PRESS

for Rodman Drake

Nothing is left. It all vanished with the dust storms. With the green parrot feathers that stuck to the drain hole, and the waterbugs that slithered back to where they had come from, and the maid's hands that switched their chicken-feather dusters from one room to another. Not even the wrought-iron balustrade remains, not the wooden banister, nor the welter of worn furniture piled up at the dead-end of the corridor.

It is all gone. Pfuif. It only exists as dusty light in my mind, a smudge of color, the musk of yellowed age in too small spaces. And then it comes back, faces floating by me, on waves, in circles, like the dreams of poisoned people, coming round and round and back, or the words to a tango that once heard are not forgot: *Qué es un soplo la vida, veinte años no es nada.* Life is but a breath, twenty years is as nothing . . .

How easy to return to that bright and dusty place—and feel, again, cool tile underfoot. And hear the music of maracas, the sound of mambos and merengues, and see the ruched and crinkled sleeves of that too hot expectant place.

THE AWAKENING

CHAPTER ONE

U p, up, up upppp," we heard from our tossed-salad beds.

"Wake up, wake up," screeched Soraida.

"Get up sleepy heads," screaked Soraida, jumping off her perch as she did every morning, taking the air while it was still thin. Because, and this is a fact of avian life, parrots prefer the cool of the night and the ease of the morning to the white blinding sun of the day. Jumping off to begin the morning's persuasions: the arousal of persons too drugged from the heat of sleep and the sulfur of dreams to know exactly what was upon them—be it fair or foul.

It took some screeching, some pecking of flesh, and a good deal of banging and slamming of slat-slanted doors for Soraida to succeed in awakening those dedicated sleepers from a slumber deeper than water.

"Up, up, up, up, upppppp!" I heard from the depths of my pillow. "Wake up, wake up. They are coming. They are coming!"

The door to our room rattled its hinges. Only a blur of bright feathery colors could I make out through the half-open slats.

"Trial day!" trilled Soraida, her vibrato bouncing against the blue walls and catching in the thick throat of that house.

"The trial is today!" sang Soraida. Crashing feet-first into our room, she tugged the sheets off my bed and nudged my linen-checked cheek with a beak the color of summer bananas.

I felt a tuft of sharp hair tickle my forehead.

"They will be here any minute!" she shouted, swirling those red radar eyes right up next to mine. "Splash your face, let's go, let's go. *Vámonos.*"

Let's go where? I thought. Who cares? What *is* this? Oh, God please let me sleep, sleep, sleep.

It was so hot.

It was always hot in that house. In that place. So hot all you could do was sleep and dream of warm things, of parrot faces streaking by you, of wings and flies and antennas and hot chocolate sauce.

That is what the heat is good for. Sleeping and growing. Growing and sleeping.

"Wake up, Goddamn it. They are coming!" Soraida squacked in my ear before hopping off once again on her grey-crinkled feet, out the door to the corridor and, who knows, beyond.

Wake up? But it was too early, far too early to do anything at all. I placed the pillow over my head. But nothing could muffle the brisk ruffling of feathers on parrot-alert—more and more screams came out of that parrot, Soraida, a crescendo of screams.

"*Chicos, chiquitas,*" she warbled and wailed. "*Vámonos.* The judges are coming: the Magistrate, the people, the mayor, the children, *todo el mundo*—and soon, soon. They are coming to judge all of you, you, the great Romandías. *Aay mi Dios.*

7

"And you are all sleeping, sleeping through the one day of your life, the one day of your life when you will be held to account for *everything.*"

I felt the shake of a door somewhere near. I heard more doors, millions of doors, all the doors in the world slat-rattling and ricocheting down the corridors. How could anyone get any sleep?

Someone sneezed in another room. Spiders vaulted to the ceiling. Alley cats scurried under the tables. I heard the tickle of tile-touching-toes skimming floors as Soraida whisked by our room on her way here and there.

"Your time has come, sleeping beauty," Soraida cooed in my ear. "Right now. Come on *niña.* Splash your face, get lively, pinch those cheeks of yours, look alert. *A mover los culitos!* They are coming, they are coming!"

Oooh. Soraida was beginning to sound like a plumed Paul Revere.

I heard more noises: the fluttering wings of unseen mosquitoes and moths and lizardy things.

Everywhere you looked in that house in the

pitiless light of day you saw one slippery creature after another so that you never quite knew what you would find when you crept into bed at night, night being when the creatures really came out and into their own—creatures with their mouths wide open and their eyes half slit sharpening their filament legs on your bedclothes, dangling upside down from your ceilings.

It was the heat, really.

It made things grow. It drove things mad, singing—*cuckoo ruu ku cooo*—fanning guitars, picking on harps, those strings percolating and dancing. *Bar-qui-si-meto, la del ritmo . . .*

"Get up Jaime," Soraida bellowed.

"Come Rico. Let's go. Come on. Time to wake up.

"You, too, Don Armando. You, too, Doña Clara." Soraida's voice boomed down that hall with its blue doors shut-faced against time and the heat.

"Come, my slumbering darlings, come now. *All* of you. *Mi dios, Madre mía, qué voy a hacer, qué puedo hacer? Mierda carajo.* The *trial* is today!"

9

∽o∾

I had forgotten about the trial. In truth I had no idea then of what a trial was or what a trial did, yet I had the vague notion that there was indeed to be one that day, the trial of my family, the Romandias of Aguas Calientes.

What did it mean? What had we done?

I knew *I* had not done anything. I was only seven years old, a *niña*, and whatever it was that I *might* have done I had not really meant to do anyway, so it did not count.

But what had *they* done? My family?

Soraida had said—when she thought that I was still asleep—that the Romandías had "fucked away the family fortune."

Maybe *that* was it.

No one could quite remember what the family fortune had been. No one ever really knew what that family of mine did—for indeed no one in that family of mine did anything.

And who could blame them? Who could work in the heat of that place in the beam of that meridional sun?

It was a useless business.

My dear father Armando had tried to work once. He imported a prize-winning Charolais bull to the port of La Guayra. He had paid what Soraida called "a lot of *lochas*" for that bull. It was going to replenish my father's fortune.

His idea was for the bull to be fruitful—to make other prize-winning bulls that he could sell at a beefy profit. All of the country would one day be populated with Charolais bulls. His bulls.

It was a business, my father crowed to us, that required no capital.

"Multiplication," said my father. "Simply multiplication."

When the bull arrived at La Guayra no one had ever heard of a Charolais so the dockworkers and stevedores renamed him Chevrolet. Chevrolet had to wait several days to pass through customs.

I went with my father to pick the Chevrolet up at La Guayra. We set off from Caracas round those treacherous trails, past green leaves wide as platters, my father's small *Citroën* hugging the red mountainsides.

We arrived at the dock and saw grand-standing ocean liners from Europe and America, and puce-colored oil tankers on their way through the Panama Canal. But look as we might, we did not see Chevrolet. Nor could the customs officers at La Guayra find a bull answering to that name—or species. They shook their heads and shrugged their shoulders—"Aiiyy," they said. "*Qué diablo.* It is a puzzle."

"But surely," my father said, raising one eyebrow. "You cannot have misplaced a ton of bull?"

The customs officers rubbed their eyes and leafed through their papers. They scratched their crotches and tongued their teeth, but still no one could produce Chevrolet—not even after my father had slipped a top-heavy tip to the head customs inspector.

They could only remember that a bull of some sort had tasted quite good—not too lean, not too fat.

Oh, people got confused. The light was so

bright. The sun was so hot. How could they have not?

It was the heat of La Guayra the stench of the petrol-filled ships, that made people hazy, made their heads light.

Why take anything seriously? *Mañana* it should be all right.

∽o∽

Trial or no trial, no one in that house ever got up until they smelled food. Not until the *arepas*, the coffee, the sweet rolls were set on the table did anyone ever arise. And most especially not my sister Grita and me, Lita. The smells had to be pretty strong before we would put our bare feet on the tile and leave our rumpled-mad beds.

Not even Soraida bestirred herself, generally speaking, unless her keen almond nostrils could dilate and circle about that sweet steaming perfume of chocolated coffee with bubbling hot milk and the white-cornmeal fragrance of gluey *arepas* and cheese. For there was nothing in the world that Soraida—that great glorious blue-and-green Guacamayo, with a beak like a prow

13

and the soul of a poet whose one great failing was a greedy response attuned mostly to food—liked as much as chocolated coffee and *arepas* and cheese.

And whereas most parrots only eat mangoes and bananas and occasionally an ugly little bug (never one that had it in him to amount to anything), Soraida had excellent taste; she had a *páladar muy fino.*

Did you know—and this is a fact well established—that parrots, like spirits, can live forever? And if parrots can live forever, Soraida at that point had already lived forever, at least she had lived forever in that hot house with its blue courtyard and tiny blue-and-white tiles on the balcony corridors and slat-covered doors and big white bathroom down the hall.

Soraida knew better than anyone else every inch of every cupboard, every particle of dust or crumb of day-old bread, every green-bellied creature, each blue-nosed apparition, every hairy black spider and brown waterbug that lived on then and there, and slinked down the wells and the holes, the cracks and the drains of that sim-mering place, where each of the creatures had its own hot pursuit of one thing or another, its own crackling tune and sizzling hot melody.

It was the heat, naturally.

It was the heat that coddled the mind and made people forget so that no one remembered where exactly Soraida had come from. She seemed to have always been there in that house in that place—before time, before me and all of us Romandías.

Always there, just like the Galápagos turtle that also went on living forever, locked up in its shell, with no quick quirky walk or spirited manner of speaking—never reading a book or thinking a thought that we knew of, just waiting for daylight or maybe for fish or for plankton or whatever it is that those types of turtles do eat.

Maybe it is all a matter of diet, why some creatures such as Soraida have more brain power while others just crawl along, never doing or say-ing a thing in their life, even if they do manage to stretch that life out to forever.

∽o∾

We lived overlooking a courtyard that contained a great many cats. They played all day long under the beds and the chairs, everywhere licking their paws with their aspery tongues, stalking birds and lizards, meowing and purring. I can still see that courtyard with cats and bright tiles and the drain hole of gold and the curving roof line of earth brick.

My Abuelita, my father's mother, put saucers of milk-soaked bread out for those lapping alley cats. Although everyone knows that once you feed a cat that cat comes back.

"*Los gatitos, los gatitos,*" Abuelita howled if anyone ever tried to shoo one of those striped scrawny creatures away. And so they stayed, dreaming always of food, surrounded by bright, rattling doors.

Everything shimmied: if you looked long enough at something in those climes, that something would start to move—to crawl or to fly. And it seems to me now that our lives were specks next to huge luminescent creatures—

creatures that twirled hot radar eyes and fanned incandescent wings.

Maybe it is the fever that makes me not forget. I am burning and I am freezing. I am going round and round.

It was so blue, the blue of celadon and quartz. And so green, the dusty green of bugs and condors.

It was like that.

Relentless.

CHAPTER TWO

Soraida was no ordinary parrot—of that I can assure you. To start with, she was extraordinary looking.

I know that looks should not be the measure of everything, but with the Romandías they just about were. So the fact that Soraida was a glorious blue and a satiny green, with a fleck of red on her shoulders and a brush-stroke of yellow on her head and a swirl of wavy black where a dimple should be, guaranteed her a place of honor in that looks-mad family of mine.

Oh, our Soraida was brilliant, all right! It was that walk of hers, that toss of the head she had, the purposeful energy in every movement she made. I could watch her for hours, going about her brisk business, pointing to this or to that, making lists, taking notes, talking often to herself.

But what made Soraida absolutely splendid was something that had little to do with the line of her beak or the color of her eyes, although that something did reside in those extraordinary lashless eyes—eyes the color of fine rubies on blue velvet.

Sentience.

This Soraida used to say again and again: beauty fades, fades like fairy gold, and all that a woman has left then is beauty of an invisible kind—the ability to be *interesante.*

Soraida herself was *interesante*, no doubt about that.

She knew—and just *how* she knew I will never know—all the corners of my mind. Nothing of me escaped her, I felt. Grita and I tried to fool Soraida plenty, tell her fibs, pull what you might call a fast one at the dinner table, dropping bits of yam and sardine and boiled chicken flesh onto the floor so that the Galápagos turtle might gulp down what we did not want.

But Soraida was instantly on to us, pecking that turtle away before it could crawl to the morsel, decrying our perfidy, our nose-running lack of respect.

And yet . . . and yet . . . Soraida was somehow divine.

Sometimes on those afternoons, when the house seemed stilled by the thickness of the very air itself, when to go out onto those high-stepped streets with the boys in their rag clothes and the corrugated doors framed in purples and reds, to walk by iron-grill windows that looked into some cooler darker place protected by crucifixes and dogs was to suspend all feeling, if and when we were not at the movies or my sister, Grita, was taking her nap, Soraida would show me, Lita, her treasures.

Out from under a bed in her room draped with fringes and thick embroideries she would pull a leather suitcase scuffed from much use. Half-shredded stickers announced that the suitcase had been to Jamaica, Trinidad, Curaçao, *La Tour Eiffel.* A large cool hasp in the shape of a butterfly spanned the case.

"Come see," said Soraida. Our cheeks

touched as we looked inside the box—its mirror reflecting our faces. On a velvet-lined tray lay small bundles cocoon-wrapped in tissue: a key, a patch of lace, a passport, even a crumbling dry candied rose that Soraida said she had plucked from the top of a wedding cake. "But do not ask me about that," she squawked at me.

There were trays inside trays inside Soraida's jewel box—all lined, like the first, in dark blue velvet. Some of them had compartments with smaller trays inside, trays with rings nestled in velvety furrows, with bracelets and lengths of necklace strewn helter skelter. Picking up each jewel, Soraida modeled her treasures, all the while telling me stories.

Soraida was almost never not talking. That was her *arte*, she said, among many of course. The art of conversation—who said what and to whom, the always and the never, without awkward pauses, or tiresome references (no politics, no religion—and certainly no quotes from Baudelaire).

"Ahh, conversation," said Soraida. "*El arte de*

la vida," an art too often discarded in a world where people plug into a box to hear what Soraida called the masturbation of conversation.

"Moreover," she pointed out, walloping the air with her beak, "conversation is an art that is always portable."

It was the blue, of course, that made people talk, talk into the night fanning themselves with their own fairy tales.

෴

Soraida told me the story of the pigeon's-blood rubies, of the starry blue sapphires, of the liquid emeralds green as the reflections of memory, jewels that had come her way hidden in bouquets of hibiscus and jasmine and orchids from her many admirers.

"Ahh," Soraida would sigh whenever she talked of some lost place of her youth, raising a bejeweled and manicured claw to her tuft-crested forehead. "Ahh," she would sigh, a slow leak of breath from her green parrot's body like the seepage from a withering balloon.

"Eur-ro-ppe," she would say, holding each

syllable on her tongue—not letting go until it had melted away with the delicacy of a communion wafer. Everything, it seemed, all the jewels, all the pleasures that were worth having and wanting, everyone that was worth knowing and loving, I was left to infer, came from "Eur-ro-ppe."

But it had been many years since Soraida herself had been back to Europe—and for this reason: a bad case of transatlantic sea-sickness, one full week of wretchedness when every meal that Soraida had tasted in the great continental cities that she so adored—the *suprême de volaile à la Caruso*, the *Funghi Porcini ala Griglia*, the *blanc mange*, the *omelette surprise* and those *Charlottes* (and Soraida pronounced that word with a liquid tenderness)—when every one of those meals had decked Soraida like a wave from a heavy sea, overcoming her with their savory poisons, had made of Soraida a land-loving parrot.

∞∞

I can feel the fever rising to my head.

Was it really like that?

Those green-tongue plants reaching for your skin? The water games of hide-and-seek and catch-me-catch-me-if-you-can?

It must have been in Europe that Soraida learned things that no lady should ever be heard to utter: *mierda* and *culo*, and *coño carajo*, *pendejo*, *especè de merde*, whoremongering mother-fuckers and all the rest of it.

Yet, given the profanity used so indiscriminately by members of the Romandía family itself in everyday speech—*puta virgen que te parió* and *anda al carajo* were routine expressions—I should say that, sprinkled as it was everywhere, Soraida's salty tongue had an effect something like parsley on a meal. Except insofar as it was used against us girls—*mocosas atrevidas* and other such signs of disaffection.

So that although Soraida had only the most refined speech, generally speaking, and was able to quote Flaubert and Balzac at the drop of a feather (her preference being for French letters, indeed for all things French), Soraida could really let go. She must have learned it all from the sailors.

"Never mind," Soraida said to me, "*where* I learned what I learned. Demand me nothing; what I know I know," she added, quoting *Othello*. "Suffice it to say, it is sometimes necessary to clear the air."

"Kill that . . . kill that . . . that . . . bird," my Abuelita would scream, clasping her hands to her ears or swinging a squawking chicken by its rubbery feet.

The three rules of success, said Soraida, were "practice, practice, practice." So practice she did. She practiced talking. She practiced singing. She practiced *poesie*.

I believe that people today are sophisticated enough to understand Soraida's poetry, but half a century ago it was wildly misunderstood. People called it disgusting, scurrilous, scatological—an insult to decent folk everywhere, a menace to public health. People just did not know any better, I guess.

And yet, when Soraida would sit on her shaded tall perch by the verandah's open doors, from which you could see the statue of Simón Bolívar in the Square, and declaim, in imitation of Edith Sitwell, her great parrot poem *Observations of Fact* or *Blowing off Steam, Version 1, 2, 3*, all the passersby on those high-stepping streets— the rag-brown little boys, the ladies with the big-bellied children hiding in the folds of their fringed and ruffled skirts, the yellow-eyed dogs with their fur full of fleas—would stop and give her their charmed attention.

I daresay, Soraida's rehearsed meditations and off-the-cuff improvisations became such a popular entertainment in those afternoons before the rains fell that at the merest squack of her voice neighbor ladies opened their wide shuttered windows and vendors stopped hawking their wares and pulled up a bench or slid into a hammock the better to drink in the cool lucubrations of Soraida, poet.

CHAPTER THREE

What in the name of the *puta virgen* do I have to do to get you Romandías ready for the trial? Who does a parrot have to fuck around here to get you girls up?"

Somehow that did it. I woke up.

What could it have been? What could it have been that my family had done? As I said, they never did anything.

My mother Clara just sat in her rocking chair. She clucked and she rocked, pressing down one foot and lifting the heel and then pressing down and lifting the other, seeming not to see anything, hear anything, just looking somewhere beyond us to whatever it was she was looking for.

My father, on the other hand, went out walking. Those temperatures made everything rise so that Don Armando, as everyone called him, could not pass a woman on those narrow, raised streets without turning to look at her, sliding his eyes over her dress, tipping his Panama hat.

When my father took Grita and me for walks to the Square, how we would skip down those streets, looking into the *cantinas* and *bodegas* full of as many flies as customers. Huge wooden doorways revealed cool shaded archways and patios. Everywhere we felt the tug of hands—begging for this, pleading for that—as we brushed by.

Was it the heat that made women take out their blue-veined breasts and nurse their babies on the street from nipples sucked as long as lozenges? Stray dogs with their teats grazing the ground zig-zagged and sniffed for scraps.

"Para hoy! Para hoy!" yelled the blind old men selling multi-colored sheets of paper lotteries that they had pinned to their clothes.

"El Diario! El Diario!" shouted the young men waving newspapers at our faces.

"A locha, a locha!" droned vendors of burnt-sugar clusters wrapped in cones of clear cellophane.

Everyone had something he needed to sell.

My father would pick a bench on the shady side of the Square, under the leathery leaves of an ancient tree, and he would slam his foot down onto a wooden shoe-shine box. We would watch as he had his shoes caressed by boys our own age who spat into their wax tins and swirled their rag-bound fingers in the melting wax. And as my father walked home in his newly shined shoes we watched again as he turned his head this way and that, waving at the Señoritas who never failed to wave back.

All my father ever did was walk and wave. That is all anyone *could* really do in that heat, with everything growing and moving. But surely that was nothing to be put on trial for. So, what was it that we could have done?

My father's younger brother Tío Jaime played chess all day long. I would see Tío Jaime scanning the worn pages of his manual, leafing through this thick, battered tome, and hear him mumble as he read to himself, playing that game of inaction in his mind, going back and forth over the chess moves until, I imagine, he had the game all perfectly played.

He had been a chess champion. He could play blindfolded. He could play backwards. Tío Jaime did not need partners. "No challenge in it," he said to his Galápagos turtle who sat by his side. "Better the manual."

"Better the chess," Soraida would say. But she never said better than what.

Maybe she meant better than anything else? As good as he was at playing chess, Tío Jaime appeared to be good at nothing else.

It was not that Tío Jaime did not try. He was always making something. For a while he made hats. Homburgs.

They were going to make his fortune, so that, he hoped, he could dedicate his life to playing chess with a manual—which he seemed to be already so good at doing. But felt Homburgs were not very popular in the tropics, where the brightness of the sun is a matter of no small concern. Those shallow brims give very little shade so that few people outside of our family ever bought Tío Jaime's hats.

Towers of fussy felt hats littered Tío Jaime's *fábrica*, pillars of bowlers fitted one into the other that mounted to the ceilings and then protruded from the windows and then tumbled down onto the cobblestone street. The people who found them used them for all sorts of things—that is, for everything except to wear on their heads.

One day Tío Jaime looked up from his manual and announced to all and sundry that from thence forward he would be using the hat factory to manufacture brassieres. "*Qué bonito!*" he said. "Imagine!"

"Imagine!" said Soraida, "Tío Jaime making brassieres in a country where women care more about the load they carry on their heads than the one that hangs from their chests."

Yet for a time Tío Jaime appeared to be very happy bringing home samples of molded brassieres that stood up and pointed all by themselves on our dining room table—and for that matter on the chairs, on the *cómoda*, dangling by their straps on the doorknobs. And Tío Jaime would smile, cupping the air with his hands, mouthing the name he had given all those brassieres: *Marilyn*.

Maybe that is why Tío Jaime never married—maybe all those molded brassieres named Marilyn gave him comfort enough. It was so hard to tell. Things were so bright that you needed to shield your eyes to see. And then what you did see was very limited.

To tell the truth nobody bought Tío Jaime's brassieres, either. But Abuelita used those brassieres the way she used anything else she could get for free—inventively—as cat bowls, bonnets, sun shades. Birds nested in them, mice had their lairs in them.

Soraida said that we were all confused.

Was *that* it? Confusion? Do they really put people on trial for that?

∞∽

"Today is the day, the trial is today," said Soraida as she pulled at my hair. "Come on," she said, pushing me to the washstand, making me splash my face it must have been a thousand times with frigid water and brush my teeth with baking soda.

I moved my head away. But Soraida held me fast by the hair. The baking soda tasted gritty like medicine. Soraida said that sometimes in this our lives we have to take the bitter with the good.

Before I could risk the *impertinencia* of asking her where was the good, she said, "*Vámonos*, Lita," and began yanking at my hair with a bristle brush, pulling it into two braids which she then coiled up—a little too roughly, now that I think about it—on either side of my head. I remember feeling a bobby pin plunged in my scalp.

"Now get dressed and I don't want to say it again," Soraida hissed, heading out the door. "I have things to do."

I heard my father's other brother, Tío Rico, shouting, "Go away, bird, what a nuisance you are. *Coño carajo* leave me alone."

Tío Rico was said to be a "great lover," although what that meant I had no clear idea and I did not dare ask Soraida. I supposed that love had something to do with music, for Tío Rico was endlessly listening to music—always the same music, tango music.

The music of the soul, said Tío Rico. So that the first thing you heard when you walked into his room was his Victrola churning out tangos like some come-up-and-see-me siren ensorcelling from a rock. And the first thing you saw was Tío Rico, his knees bent, plunging and swerving all by himself in front of the mirror, dipping some imaginary *mujer* in his arms.

All around the room there were rows of neatly displayed Japanese dolls with white-bisque faces, their hair all combed a shiny black, their lips vermilion red, their heads bouncing up and down—dolls that Tío Rico had once tried to sell.

Sometimes the air was so heavy that Tío Rico would be wearing only a ribbed cotton undershirt tucked into his pants, and I could see a field of sparse curly hair sprouting from his chest.

And every one of those hairs, I was sure, danced to the music.

If he was particularly moved, Tío Rico would bury his dark head in his arms and warble and shake like a newborn bird.

"Remembering old loves," Tío Rico explained, as he looked at his profile in the mirror above his dresser and combed his hair with a flat-handled brush. "Ahhh love, *chiquita*, *mi vieja*," he crooned, jutting his chin out as far as it would go.

"Ahhh, what a profile," said Tío Rico patting his hair with brilliantine. "What a good-looking uncle you have!"

And then he looked straight at me and said, "Lita, never get married. It spoils everything. But if you do, promise me you will never wear your husband's socks to bed at night. *Prométeme*."

35

Love was silly, I thought, if it made grown men wail over phonograph records. But then Soraida had said that Tío Rico had never grown up, that that was his problem, because all he ever did was listen to infernal tango music. God knows, he was old enough to have grown up by now.

"Trying to sing a tango," Soraida said, "he sounds like a wounded coyote—you cannot imagine how much he makes those of us gifted with perfect pitch suffer.

"Ever notice," asked Soraida, "that the human affliction is to get up and sing? No matter how insufficient the natural talent, humans ache to be singers. The whole musical firmament is in a tailspin. Actors who should know better leap up to the stage not to recite Shakespeare but to belt out a toneless tune.

"And comedians—they are the worst offenders. In between the jokes they sing. Why don't they just leave the songs to the singers?"

And that maid of ours, Hortensia Salsipuedes, singing arias from Puccini no less, blares *forte fortissimo* as she goes from room to room dragging her mop and sloshing that pail. "Those with the least natural talent," said Soraida, "are the first to flaunt it. It is an axiom."

Perhaps Tío Rico's talents lay elsewhere, I argued. He was certainly a good listener. Moreover, for a person who was not a grown up Tío Rico had produced quite a few children—at least eight.

That took talent.

Although I knew it was the heat that made everything multiply, the heat combined with the rain.

Those Tío Rico children came calling, in unison, through the big iron gate, but then they scattered all over the house as fast as the bugs— swishing their ruched cotton dresses, twirling the big blue bows in their hair. I must say, they looked very pretty as they held their hands up over their heads and jigged.

Tío Rico carried them on his shoulders or

under his arms, depending on how heavy they were. Oh, there were so many of them. Lana. Rita. Hedy. Dolores. Greta. Ava . . .

But those children with the movie-star names, Soraida explained to me, were not really Tío Rico's. They belonged to God the Father, since their mother was not Tío Rico's wife, since Tío Rico was unmarried as yet, so that his children were, technically speaking, not his at all and were therefore referred to by all of us as not real.

Tío Rico had children who were Chinese. Maybe that is why they were not real.

Well, not real like *we* were real—that is, us girls:

Me, Lita, short for Angelita and my sister, Grita, short for horrible-screamer-witch-child-nuisance.

My sister, Grita, was real all right, that I can tell you.

CHAPTER FOUR

My sister, Grita, was wheezing in the bed next to mine with a chicken feather caught in her sticky nostril— the chicken feather fluttering up and down like a saxophone valve. She was a very noisy sleeper. She was a very noisy person. She was a famously noisy person. Famous at least in those parts for taking the hush off those afternoons with her tantrums.

Soraida said, among other wise and terrible things, that my sister Grita needed housebreaking. And Soraida should know as it was her province to educate and edify the two of us girls. We had never been to school—at least to what other people might think of as school, with teachers and classmates and desks with wooden benches.

As a consequence of our . . . well . . . ignorance if you must, it fell to Soraida, whose educational experience was far-flung, to ensure that we learned how to, for instance, read.

I had a small paper-bound book. It had illustrations captioned with bold-faced words divided into proper syllables. Every morning I had to recite for Soraida the word that I read under the picture of a bird in a bird cage: "*PA-JA-RO, pa-ja-ro, pa-ja-ro.* Bird."

While I recited my lessons, Grita would be under the table pulling on the tail of one of the alley cats or licking the floor tiles. Soraida would get angry when Grita recited not what she was reading—because read she could not—but whatever it was she imagined was written under the illustration, which in every case could not have been further from the truth; so she said: "*PA-JA-RE-RA.* Bird cage!"

When Soraida insisted time had come for her studies, Grita would run down the hall and lock herself in the big bathroom with the cranky washing machine that stood in the middle of the floor. That bathroom was where the biggest of the waterbugs lived. Grita and I would stalk them there, and then crack their waxy chocolate shells with the point of a stick and watch their gluey insides ooze out.

Grita wailed that she would commit suicide if she had to do her lessons. She said she had a knife on her and that she was going to use it! Soraida tried to coax Grita out, cooed all manner of sweet things to her, promising her trips to the zoo and candy bars aplenty and all the cavity causing sodas she could ever possibly drink.

But I could see through the slats of the door that the knife Grita had was only a dinner knife —and one without serrated edges.

Soraida said that it was important to be *educada*. That young ladies needed to be *educadas* to find nice husbands and get good homes. But Grita said that she wanted to stay stupid, that she had no use for things like husbands and homes.

Soraida shook her head vigorously. *"Que mierda,"* she said, "that child, that child! What have I ever done to deserve a child like that?"

Our maid Hortensia Salsipuedes—who herself had a reputation of sorts for her devil-worshipping *brujerías* what with the rancid olive oil she used to braid her black Indian hair—told me in confidence, *"entre nosotras,"* that my sister was a witch-child.

Hortensia Salsipuedes said she *knew* Grita was a witch-child, because Grita had yellow eyes and pointy teeth and hair like wire snakes.

It was the rain, of course. The rain that made my sister's hair grow frizzly and up instead of down.

The rains fell every afternoon at the same time so that what had been bright became instantly dark. It would rain so hard and so loud that creatures would crawl up the sashaying palm fronds to where they could stay dry, and people would run on their crusted feet along the cobblestone streets into the courtyards where the tiles were still wet and slick from the day before.

Heat and rain. Day and night. Hortensia Salsipuedes slap-slapping down the halls into rooms with beds unmade and pillows punched and thrown.

Hortensia Salsipuedes knew a great deal about witches, she-devils, he-devils and other *espíritus* from beyond the beyond. Hortensia Salsipuedes could hide herself at will in the walls of that house—and, believe me, those walls were thick. She could become invisible to all of us, and then step right out of a wall whenever she felt like it.

One day, while we were playing hide-and-seek, Hortensia Salsipuedes walked into the wall, vowing not walk out of it until I gave up. I heard her say from somewhere, "Give up? Give up?" and when I said, "Yes!" she emerged laughing in triumph, from the kitchen wall.

Hortensia Salsipuedes had seen the Devil. "*Oh sí niña. Como no*," she told me. She insisted that she had definitely seen him one night when she was all tucked in bed, saying her rosary, turning the beads in her fingers and, if that time was like any of the other times when I had

43

seen Hortensia Salsipuedes, she was probably flattening and rubbing her chest with her palms. Possibly, she admitted, she was reciting her rosary a little too quickly for she had had a good deal to drink and was feeling very *disipada* that night. And it was then that the Devil materialized to torment her.

The Devil was a headless, hairless dog running in circles around the room, dripping blood. It was not a lovely sight. *"Nada bonito,"* said Hortensia Salsipuedes, handing me a magic card to ward off the Devil.

"Keep it under your pillow, *niña,*" she advised.

On one side of the card was a calendar which, if you held up and inclined it at a certain angle, became a picture of a gas station. On the other side was a gold-edged image of the *Virgen del Fátima.* It was the *Virgen,* of course, not the gas station, that was meant to protect me from evil and I supposed in particular from evil as incarnated by the witch-child my sister.

Soraida said that Hortensia Salsipuedes was

an ignorant Indian and that I was to pay no heed to her ramblings unless I, too, wanted to find my head full of hairless-dog spittle.

Still, I found myself listening to Hortensia Salsipuedes's tales and admonitions of "*el mundo del más ayá*" out of something more than politeness. To this day I wonder if Hortensia Salsipuedes did not know more about *el mundo* than an unforgotten parrot by the name of Soraida gave her credit for.

CHAPTER FIVE

I felt the coolness of the tile under my feet as I stood on the gallery.

Soraida was setting the table, laying the forks and the knives and the big tablespoons at each place, shooing away the cats, swiping at the lizards.

"*Qué mierda*," I heard her muttering. "*Pendejada.*"

Then Soraida shouted, "Hortensia, Hortensia!" Before I knew it, Soraida was in the courtyard flushing Hortensia Salsipuedes from behind the kitchen where she slept.

"Come on now," she said. "Hurry up. *Vámonos. Vamos.* The trial is today."

I walked to the balustrade and peered down at Hortensia Salsipuedes, still in her faded striped bathrobe and flop-back slippers. She

46

looked as if she had not yet washed her face or brushed her teeth. Yet something Soraida whispered in her ear seemed to awaken her and she went back into the kitchen and emerged with a pointy tail broom.

With a vigor I had never seen any evidence of before Hortensia Salsipuedes began sweeping the courtyard, in that motion of hers so familiar to me—beginning at the outer reaches of a room and then sweeping in inner-directed circles until dead in the center of the floor a neat pile of dust and cracked clay was formed, which Hortensia Salsipuedes could pick up with her leathery fingers.

I could hear a low murmur—Hortensia Salsipuedes muttering something to herself or to someone or something I could not see, lodged deep in her superstition-ridden brain, her bathrobe sliding open under the hemp rope she used for a belt. The rope slid under her belly, which stuck out from her thin frame like a pimento-stuffed olive impaled on a toothpick. *Flaca, fané y descangallada.*

"*Más rápido, rápido,*" cried Soraida.

"*Ya voy. Ya voy,*" replied Hortensia Salsipuedes, finishing her sweeping and scraping off bird droppings with smashed black nail. Hortensia Salsipuedes scooted back and forth to the kitchen, dragging pieces of furniture out to the courtyard: metal folding chairs, an old table that was new to me, caked with pastry dough and chicken feathers. She placed the table under the fat tree at one end of the courtyard and set the chairs up around it.

Then Hortensia Salsipuedes climbed the steps to our shaded balcony overlooking the courtyard and slid past me to the open-air table where we took all our meals.

The chickens in the kitchen began to squawk. I heard them banging up against their pens. The water bugs came out of hiding and then slipped back down into their wells and holes and cracks. The alley cats slinked under the tables.

It did not take long for the smell of sweet rolls and butter, of hot chocolated coffee, of

48

foaming milk, to percolate through the long, tall corridors, to waft through the louvered doors, licking our nostrils with the irresistible perfume of breakfast.

My Abuelita came out of her room; a white dust cloud popped out behind her. My father opened and closed his door. More doors opened and closed.

Tío Jaime slipped out of his room with his thumb in his chess manual, and sang "HAA-TAAAH," the way he did every morning.

"Worshipping the sun," said Tío Jaime, blowing the air out of his lungs in a wooosh.

Small, blue-tinged birds with whirring wings alighted on his head. One of the alley cats clawed at his leg trying to reach the birds. But Tío Jaime kept droning: "Oooo hhhh mmmm."

He had what Soraida called "great concentration." He stood balanced on one leg, shaking the other as if a bunch of birds and a stalking cat were just so many flies and moths.

"They are just little bitty things," he would say. "You can eat them if you want. See?" And he

49

would squeeze a green bug between his fingers and lick up the smoosh. "Delicious," Tío Jaime pronounced.

I once watched a fat green caterpillar condensing itself up the side of the wall. "Let me," said Tío Jaime. Then he doused the poor caterpillar with canned kerosene and dropped a lit kitchen match on him. You could smell him roasting. Tío Jaime said he tasted better cooked.

I know it was the green that made him do that. The green of caterpillars and ferns and broken sea-glass of rotten teeth and filmy evil eyes, and of turtles sliding one flippery foot ahead of the other.

Tío Jaime's Galápagos turtle came to a full stop at Tío Jaime's feet and raised its loose withered head. Tío Jaime just shook his leg—the cat still clinging to it—at the turtle.

Soraida sat on her gnarled perch next to the dining table. She was arching her back, letting the muscles ripple in waves, and humming a tune to herself. Suddenly, tail feathers fanning straight up, eyes swirling she cried:

"*Qué tengo qué hacer? Qué puedo hacer?* What need I do to get you all up, for once, *desayunados*, just this once. *Mon Dieu, Mon Dieu!* Is there not one grain of sense in those sun-addled heads? THE TRIAL IS TODAY."

Tío Rico bolted out of his room and flew down the hall, his silk bathrobe winging out behind him: "I get the bathroom fiiirrrsssst."

"Eat, eat," Soraida was saying to me, holding my nose until I opened my mouth, with her beak pushing bits of soft buttered bread down my throat.

"Sit down, Grita, my girl, sit down," she said as my sister appeared.

Grita dilated her nostrils in the direction of the steam emanating from the large platter of *arepas* that Hortensia Salsipuedes was in the process of bringing to the table. Slick as a lizard's tongue her hand reached out to grab an *arepa*. She put the corn cake full square in her mouth and chomped it down.

"They will be here any minute," said Soraida jumping up and down from her perch.

"Oh so what?" I thought, "Let them come. Who cares?"

I did not know.

All I knew was that rolls, guava jelly, *arepas* melting with cheese were set on the table, that Tío Jaime was singing "Haaa-taaah," that Tío Rico was off preening in the bathroom, and that Abuelita was dousing herself with dust.

And then suddenly my father appeared.

CHAPTER SIX

Actually, the smell of my father's fruit-laced cologne preceded him.

There was not a day of his life— that I can remember—when he did not splash on some imported *extraflagrante* cologne and slick back his dark thinning hair with the gelatinous *pomada Verde de Rosas* that he so adored. The whole of my father was slicked and *perfumado*, ever ready for some *baile* or *fiesta* or any gathering of *chicos* and *chicas*.

This day he was dressed in a white linen suit. The creases in the pants were straight as razor blades. He wrist-flicked his straw sombrero onto a chair and, with barely a glance at my sister, Grita, and me, and not even a nod for Soraida, my father took his place at the head of the table.

"*Buenos días*, Doña Soraida," he said, shaking out his napkin. "What is all the *vulla* about?"

Before Soraida could answer, my father clapped his hands together and inclined his face expectantly, indicating that he was ready to be served.

Hortensia Salsipuedes darted out of the kitchen, hot coffee pot in one hand, steaming milk pot in the other, and bowing *buen día* to my father, placed before him a soup-sized cup of coffee, with precisely the right proportion of coffee to milk—my father was a very particular man.

He could tell just from the look of the thing, from the absence of steam misting over its surface, or from the way the bubbles curled on the edge of the cup, that the *café con leche* in question was not *caliente* enough, so that Hortensia Salsipuedes was always on full alert—she might at any second be called upon to go slipslopping back to the kitchen to fetch coffee so hot, so very *caliente*, that it would scald the roof of any mouth.

"*Huevos*, Hortensia," my father announced. "*Huevos fritos*."

My father was particular about his eggs, too: They should not be too soft, or too runny, and certainly never greasy. Nor could they be too translucent, though they should also not be too opaque. That morning, I recall, my father sent those fried eggs back because they were "look here, too wrinkled."

"One moment please," Soraida pronounced between beakfuls of coffee and chomps of *arepa*, "just one more morsel first," said Soraida, pecking off another sticky chew of *arepa*. "The trial, Don Armando, is *today*."

My father was inspecting the two fried eggs on his plate. "Yes, yes, of course," he said distractedly. "What do you take me for, Doña Soraida?"

I saw Soraida bite her lower lip.

Suddenly my father looked up from his plate and clapped his hands again, full and loud, one long and two short claps. "Hortensia, Hortensia, look here, too filmy."

Soraida sucked in her cheeks, closed her eyes and let her wavy head fall back on the ledge of her shoulders. "Don Armando, please, I implore you to remember the parchment you received the other day, the one with the wax seal—and the magistrate who delivered it to you by hand?"

"So?" asked my father. "What of it?"

"So? Today is it—judgment day, the day they are coming to judge you, *you*. You and your entire family, all the Romandías."

"Ahgh, just tell them I am away on a trip —abroad," said my father, slathering a toasted round of bread with guava jelly.

"No, better yet," he went on, looking around at us with the touch of a smile on his face. "Tell them that we are all abroad, all on a trip, a trip of indefinite duration!"

"Don Armando," said Soraida. "You cannot tell the Magistrate and the judges that you are all away when it is patently obvious that you are all very much still here. The Magistrate and the judges are not going to be turned away by obfuscation at the door. They will demand entry—and then what?"

My father held up to general view a bit of bread dough that he had been kneading under the table. "Guess what this is?" he asked. "Girls, can you tell? Come on, Lita, what do you think?"

"A salamander?" I answered.

"No. No. Ooh. Oooh, let me. Let me. I know. I know," Grita insisted. "A bird!"

"How right you are," said my father beaming. "See the beak," he said pointing at the bit of dough, "and the body? Pretty good, eh? I should have been a sculptor. What do you think, Doña Soraida?"

"Please, Don Armando!" implored Soraida fluttering her ruff wings in what can only have been exasperation.

"I do not think it polite, Doña Soraida," said my father, winking at Grita and me, "to discuss weighty matters at table. It is bad for the gastric juices, an impediment to their timely flow. And certainly, it will not do to discuss serious matters at table without my sainted wife and mother present."

As if my father had conjured her up from inside the yellow orbs of the two egg yolks at which he now sat glaring, Abuelita slid to the table trailing a halo of white dust that danced brightly in the early-morning sun-rays.

"Good morning, everyone," she intoned. "Fine morning *niñas*, is it not?" Holding back the sleeve of her satiny kimono, she reached for the sweet rolls with a bony hand.

Abuelita had her seaweed hair up in two brioche-braids coiled into place on either side of her head. Hatpins stuck out from these braids and though she was in fact very old, her hair was still lustrous-black.

It must have been the mud. Abuelita liked to sit in mud. It made her young again, she said. We all went to the thermal baths where people sat caked in mud and the air smelled of sulfur. We ate pulpy fruit with jelly-coated seeds that spilled down our faces while prickly melons dropped from their branches and burst their rotten red insides out onto the ground.

It was the blue that made Abuelita sit in mud and bathe in spider's milk and flutter chicken-feather eyelashes. Those lashes clung to her brow-bone but nowhere near the lash-line because Hortensia Salsipuedes had to glue them on for her and neither one of them could see. It was just too bright to see.

"Grita," Abuelita was saying. "Please do not eat with your mouth open. Jaime stop that singing and come sit here next to mama, mama who loves you so much."

"Revolting display of maternal affection," whispered Tío Rico in my ear as he finally sat down at the table. "I bet you are still a virgin? Am I right?"

I did not answer him. Tío Rico was always asking such impertinent questions. Soraida said that all that tango dancing had left Tío Rico with an impairment—a bend in the knees so pronounced that he was permanently crouched.

This impairment, she said, had pulled Tío Rico's brain down into his knee caps.

There was a great deal of noise. It was my mother. She slumped down in her rocking chair opposite my father, her arms and legs flailing.

"Ah, Clara," said my father.

My mother's eyes looked closed. I could see her trying to raise one of her eyelids with the arch of her brow, but the eyelid had other ideas.

"Ca, caf," my mother was saying, cradling the large coffee cup in front of her face. She wheezed a slow steady stream of sleepy air. Hortensia Salsipuedes seemed to have understood whatever it was that my mother was saying, for she filled my mother's coffee cup with foaming *café con leche*.

"Aaaagggghhhhhh!" Soraida screamed. "I do not believe this. Today is your judgment day. I have never seen an assortment of ill-prepared, irresponsible lazies to match this one."

"Oh, come on, Soraida deary," drawled Tío Rico through his broadest smile. Tío Rico had a fine set of glistening teeth. "That is not so very nice of you, is it? I have not finished my *arepa* yet."

"You take care of it," said my father.

"What do you mean, 'You take care of it?'" Soraida shrieked.

"I mean, *you* handle it," said my father. "I could not be any clearer, now, could I?"

"Why in *coño* hell should I handle it?" asked Soraida. "It is *your* trial. You are the alleged perpetrators. I am just an innocent bystander!"

"I would not be so sure if I were you," said my father. "What about those Sitwellian meditations of yours that have the neighbors all aflutter?"

"Can't you see we are all too tired to do anything?" asked Tío Rico.

"Yes, and I have to study my chess," said Tío Jaime. "I have an important game to play tomorrow."

"And I want to play jacks," said Grita, chewing with her mouth open, "and pull the wings off waterbugs."

"And I'm too busy in the kitchen," said Hortensia Salsipuedes.

Abuelita powdered herself with more dust.

My mother said nothing: she let her head fall forward, and began to snorkel in the *café con leche*. Luckily, the cup was very wide.

"*Por favor,*" said my father. "Soraida, please. I appeal to you on bended knees. You are the only one of us awake enough, lucid and skilled enough, to take on a tribunal. We are all . . . ," and here my father paused, "we are all dreamers."

Now, Soraida was certainly the finest parrot that I have ever known or likely ever will—exquisitely attuned to the feelings of others, but though she had only the loftiest manners, that morning she disgorged a cacophony of expletives not wildly appropriate to a family setting—there was a lot of fucking, *mierda*, *coño carajo*, *puta* mothers, *culo*, cocks, *pendejos*, and pendant testicles, bursting forth full-throated from her beak in a crescendo so loud that no one quite noticed the noise from the street.

CHAPTER SEVEN

Soraida was raging still—"*mierda carajo, pendejos*"—when we heard the infernal noise. Yet my father and mother, Abuelita, Tíos Rico and Jaime just sat at the table, passing the rolls from one to the other, unheeding, unperturbed by the thundering outside.

Grita and I ran together to the verandah that fronted on the street. Booming and cartwheeling above us we saw detonations of red, green, blue.

Fireworks at that hour?

Everything anyway was topsy-turvy.

Grita and I leaned out over the verandah in our impatience to discover what was what, and what was not. With the balls of our bare feet wedged between the balusters, we made out in the squint-eyed grey-blue morning light of those circles roiling above us, something common-place but strange, something ordinary but extraordinary—a plumed donkey pulling a cart.

My father had told us in one of those many moments when he reminisced about Life before Mother—which life was varied and long—of a trip he had made to Mexico, intending to stay for a week. He stayed seven years. It was there, canoeing with Señoritas on the flower-boughed waterways of Xothchimilco and drinking *agua-fuerte* in the *cantinas*, that he managed to learn a thing or two about donkeys.

Mexico, my father told us, is a country one leaves only with great effort. My father stayed on in a tiny boarding house with raspberry walls and pink bougainvillea growing through the windows. And every morning he awakened to the braying of a donkey. He told us quite authoritatively that there was no sound quite so lovely. And that ever since then that song of a donkey reminded him only of beautiful women and skies full of love.

But the donkey my sister and I saw coming

down the street the morning of our trial and trib-
ulations was not braying. The *burrito*'s carrot ears
twitched tight tiny circles and its glazed grena-
dier eyes stared straight ahead. And though it
must have been hard for that lone silent donkey
to pull that clattering cart over the cobblestone
street, the animal was moving with seeming pur-
pose and dispatch—the cart wheels hopped and
listed into the ruts.

Now, on that street of blue-washed walls
and open doorways and filigreed windows, Grita
and I were used to seeing all sorts of *cosas*: ven-
dors from near and far, dogs without fur, cats on
fire . . .

There were showbirds that performed on the
improvised stages of vegetable crates turned up-
side down on the street. The extravagant Lorenzo
the *Sábelo Todo* would retrieve paper fortunes
from a box for a *locha*, and scribe-birds would, for
a fee, memorize a message and deliver it to a
loved one far away.

And then there were the avian vocalizers—
the orators and singers: the Mynas, Loritos and

Loros, Tucanes, Guacamayos, each one speaking—or squawking—his piece.

But for all the creatures whose startling acquaintance Grita and I had made on that cobblestoned street we had never seen a donkey and cart like the one we saw that morning.

A pink plume trembled on the donkey's topknot; its black leather blinders kept it looking straight ahead. Above the cart was a sign the size of a movie marquee. "JUSTICE," it read. Justice! The letters shimmered and shimmied.

Underneath the word "justice" was written in letters smaller and steadier yet still luminescent:

"Traveling Circuit Court—Justice and Retribution For All."

The donkey and cart came to a halt in front of where my sister and I were standing and shaking on the verandah. The sign very definitely said "JUSTICE."

It was only then that I noticed the cart had a driver, a man who, save for the gold of his sunglasses and the glint of gold edging his teeth, ab-

sorbed all the available light. His shirt, jodh-
purs, belt and hair—not to mention the cigar he
was puffing on—were all brown. The man was
wearing boots punished to the highest gloss.

He seemed the sort of person who, I dis-
tinctly recall thinking then, *does not like children*.
He appeared to be checking a piece of paper that
he held in his hand. He looked up at us and then
down at the street number at the side of our
door; he clicked his gold-edged teeth and shook
the donkey reins that he held slack in his hands.
Then donkey and cart came on up towards our
verandah, heading for our front door.

Grita and I sped back into the house, slap-
ping those cool floors with our feet as we ran, try-
ing not to upset the bowls of milk left out for
the cats.

We ran through the velvety darkness of the
draped dining room, and beyond it to the shaded
alcove where we had all our meals, and up to the
balustraded balcony that ran along the interior
length of the house, overlooking the open court-
yard.

And there right below us, circling in and around the shiny tile floors were—unmistakably, inescapably—that cart and that donkey, and that driver.

The animal's lips were curling, revealing big bold teeth like yellowed piano keys. And if a donkey could possibly look full of itself, that donkey that morning looked to me even smug. I thought that any minute it would start to crow! And indeed, it did begin to bray. But what a sound it was that came out of it! It was not a beautiful song, not a beautiful song at all, not a song of love or of azure skies or of the swishing of petticoats. I had to confront the possibility that my father had not told us the whole truth about donkeys.

The donkey's tune was an unpleasant low-nasal note—the sound of a rusty duck horn.

The chickens in the kitchen began to squawk, thumping again on their wire pens. The water bugs came out of hiding—only to think better of it and slip back down into their wells and holes and cracks.

But my sister and I just crouched, pressing our faces through the hand-gripped balustrade, staring at that pink-plumed donkey, its cart and its *caca*-brown-clothed driver.

The man stepped to the back of the cart and drew aside a green velvet curtain. Three men jumped out, and I remember thinking that it must have been hot in there.

They were little men—no taller than Grita and me—and, it seemed to me then, un-*importante*-looking. If I had not known better, I would have guessed that they were the *verdulero*, the chickencoop keeper, and the former companion of Hortensia Salsipuedes, who was said to be some kind of chauffeur.

While the driver tied the donkey's rein to the foot of our stairs, the three men began pulling things out of the cart: a pile of clothes, a lectern, four chairs, a bag of white cotton, some wooden benches, and three huge gilt-edged books, each one bound in a different color, which they handled with great care.

For the time being, the driver simply sat in

the corner of our courtyard chewing on a cigar. He was licking it all around the edges with a slippery tongue that I was sure was as brown as everything he wore and the cigar was getting wetter and wetter and darker and darker. Every once in a while he spat out of the side of his mouth into one of the fern cans.

One of the little men motioned to the driver to come over and help set up a table. The driver slipped the wet cigar into a special cigar flap on his brown breast-pocket and then stooped to put his two hands under the table's corners.

Another of the little men licked his finger and stuck it up in the air, cocked his head in the direction of this finger erectus, and glanced sideways at where my sister and I were watching from above. He seemed satisfied, for he motioned with a sweep of his arm to the two other little men.

All of them then converged on a spot at the far end of the courtyard—the shadiest spot, as it happened, where the tiles on the wall and the floor were the darkest ultramarine—a spot near one of Abuelita's favorite plants, a flat, lazy fern.

It must have been the green of those plants that lived in their tins with the heat trapped inside them that made those three little men converge on our courtyard and say neither boo nor thank you nor even hello-how-are-you.

The whole while we were watching, the men talked among themselves, gesticulating violently and then calming down. They hauled and adjusted and dragged all of the things they had brought with them, placing the tables in a row in the corner, the clothes in a mass on the floor. Finally they seemed pleased by the arrangement of benches and stopped their work.

It was then that one of them pulled out from his sack a thermos of coffee and a greasy brown paper bag, which was full of *arepas*. Keeping one for himself, he passed the rest to the others.

One whiff of that glutinous cornmeal, one snort of that aromatic coffee was all that it took for Soraida to spring onto the banister of the balcony and heaving her bosoms—for Soraida had a highly developed sense of the dramatic—stretch out her plumed cape to its widest—and plunge full-breasted and full-throated to the courtyard below, looking like Daedalus riding toward the sun.

In the most imperious—nay, imperial—manner and tone she could muster, Soraida exclaimed:

"Just what in hell do you no-goodnicks think you are doing here?" And then as we held our breath, she added in the immortal words of another great diva, "Don't fuck with me, boys."

CHAPTER EIGHT

t was more than Soraida could bear, I knew, to watch those three little men chewing their *arepas*, impervious to her query, and since *arepas* can be as chewy as they can be sticky particularly if they are not properly cooked— which those *arepas* demonstrably were not—the three little men just kept on chewing, picking their teeth now and then with the ends of their pinkie-nails. Soraida did always say that one could tell the exact breeding of a person from the way he eats.

This was more than Soraida could or would endure. She swooped down on the men, who were now wiping the crumbs off their chins with the backs of their hands and exploring the front of their teeth with the tips of their tongues.

"Revolting," she said. "Unspeakable," she

added. *"Degôutant!"* she pronounced. *"Asquero-sos!"* she shouted, flapping her wings indignantly, ruffling her feathers all in a rush, barely touching the ground with her long, crinkled toes.

"Qué mierda business do you have being in our courtyard?" she demanded of them. "What greasy low-life kind of *guacho atrevido,"* she exploded, "would dare to sit here in front of a lady eating *arepas* and cheese, unannounced and uninvited? Who would have the effrontery to sit in this courtyard, *my* courtyard *our* courtyard," she gestured to us, "perfect strangers, and eat with their filthy mouths open?"

The three little men seemed amused or, if you will, unruffled. The driver who until now had managed to go unseen by the normally all-seeing Soraida, so busy was she fuming at the three and their cornmeal, stood up and without saying a word, but merely strutting the gilt in his teeth, moved over to where she had just flourished her wings and flapped her mouth. In one swift deft maneuver he trapped and imprisoned Soraida in a large butterfly net.

"What, what," she sputtered, trying to extricate her green-and-blue parrot body from the web of netting. But her high beautiful words and even her low, profane ones failed her, and all that her slug-slippery tongue could find to say was: "You have some nerve! Let me out of here! Rape! Rape!"

The driver grinned and said in a voice pitched threateningly low, "Now, now, my dear Madam, I believe you have been expecting us." Here he paused and looked up at us. "You certainly have the right to remain silent. You have the right to an attorney. You have a lot of rights but for the moment they are null and void and therefore useless. And you, my dear feathered lady, and in fact all of you," he looked up again, "are under house arrest."

"House arrest?" Grita did not know what it meant. I told her it was like homework.

"House arrest? By what right? By what

right?" asked Soraida, raising her color-drained face against the netting.

By now the commotion had fully awakened everyone in the house—Abuelita, my father, my mother, my Tíos Rico and Jaime, Hortensia Salsipuedes. We all stood at the banister as if posing for a family snapshot but staring into nowhere.

Could this be what Soraida had been squawking about all morning? Was this the trial?

For the first time we saw the driver clearly, full-face.

"Good morning my friends," he addressed us, the gold in his teeth reflecting klieg-like rays of sun as he talked. "Allow me to introduce myself. I am Oscar Vargas, Chief Magistrate of our glorious town of Aguas Calientes. You must recognize me, no? From my picture?"

I did then recall that on the wall behind the meat counter the butcher kept a picture that did sort of resemble this man. The man in the picture wore a gold-trimmed *sombrero* and plenty of gold braids on his shoulders, but nowhere near the number of gold chains, medallions, and tassels that the President of the Republic wore in *his* official portrait. Why, the President of the Republic had gold on his visor and gold on his scabbard and gold in his gloves!

"And here I am, in your courtyard, which, compliments to you, Señora," Oscar Vargas went on, tipping his cap in the direction of my mother, "is so lovingly kept."

With a nod to the three little men he had come with, Oscar Vargas continued, "These are my esteemed colleagues and my very dear friends, the three Justices of the Traveling Circuit Court. Señores Triste, Redondo y Caliente. Take a bow, all of you, please."

The three men bowed at the waist.

"And now by the powers vested in me and in us, by the state, by the city, by his Excellency the Plenipotentiary President of the Republic, most extraordinary, and by my office of Magistrate, we are come to place you, Romandías one and all, under arrest. And we place you, Soraida, Parrot *Extraordinaria*, also under arrest." Oscar Vargas raised his tiny eyes to all of us. "You family of birdbrains and foul-mouthed birds, you benighted blights on humanity, you indolent dust collectors, you are all under arrest as of this moment."

With that, Oscar Vargas turned abruptly around. The justices licked from their fingers the last gluey bites of *arepas* with cheese, tossed the soiled paper wrappers and napkins on the floor, and proceeded, successively, with the ordering of chairs, the stacking of books, and the donning of robes.

"Release me! Release me, you Robespierres!" cried Soraida.

"This is an outrage," my father repeated, standing almost on the tips of his toes. "This is impossible."

"This is a calumny!" said Soraida.

"This is . . . is. . . . Is," said Tío Rico.

"Really?" said Oscar Vargas. "What is . . . is, is. The wonder is that we did not come a long time ago."

And turning in the direction of one of the justices, he ordered, "Let the spectators in."

The justice went to the big double wooden doors shaded in the arch of the entrance that led out onto the street, and with some effort managed to push open first the one door and then the other.

And at this, a procession of women and old men on canes, of hairless dogs, and of children with bellies round as balloons, their tummy buttons squiggling like slugs on a leaf, of prelates in scruffy burlap robes and nuns in habits starched and winged, and even of a group of sable-lined rabbis—all these came scurrying in, and soon our courtyard was filled with their intrusive bodies.

I noticed that some—mostly the older ones —had brought along folding stools, along with packed lunches, fans, and radios that buzzed and cackled as they spun the dials. Others sat cross-legged on the floor or lay down, leaning on one elbow. I saw a few of them step on Abuelita's plants in the coffee tins. "Watch your fat feet," Abuelita yelled down from the balustrade. "Can't you see?" We girls were never allowed even to touch any of Abuelita's dusty plants as they yawned in the sun.

Without warning, Grita started to cry. She flung herself forward and we caught her as she hooked her toes over the banister of the verandah. Grita was hanging upside down like a bat. She lifted one foot and dangled like a pair of open scissors. You could see the tiny dolls printed on her cotton bloomers trimmed in eyelet lace. Her wiry hair was curling up toward the railing. She lifted both feet and held on by her hair, not knowing, it seemed to me then, whether she wanted to laugh or cry or scream or what.

Then she cried, "Soraida!"

Hooked by foot and hair, she screamed as loudly as she could scream, "Soraida!" Spittle collected in her mouth; droplets fell on people in the courtyard.

Grita's screams were so loud I was sure that they could be heard from one end of the country clear to the other. In Barquisimeto, in Carúpano, in Maracaibo, in the low wet plains and in the Gran Sabana. They were so loud I imagined that even radio stations picked up her signals and carried her screams, her crackling "Soraida!" melding with static or guitar music.

She was a practiced—and accomplished—screamer.

Then as suddenly as she had started to cry, Grita started to laugh, and that is when she fell off the verandah onto the spectators below.

CHAPTER NINE

H ouse arrest, what an outrage!" my father said. "And to think that I made a hefty contribution to that vile Magistrate's campaign."

"It couldn't have been much money," my Abuelita interrupted, patting her face with white powder from a chicken feather puff.

Tío Jaime looked up from his chess manual and clicked his teeth. He must have had something caught between his incisors.

"Now, let me think," said my father waving his open hand in the air like royalty. "What *are* we to do?"

My father turned away from the banister and sat back down at the breakfast table. He cradled his pomaded head in both hands. "Soraida was going to handle this," my father said, "and now she's stuck down there with those peasants," and here my father lowered his voice, "those *criminals*." Collecting himself he added, "I don't mind telling you that I don't like the look of this, not one bit."

"Who's looking?" demanded my Abuelita. "We have to do something *mijito*, and *ahorita*. We need Soraida up here slippery slick, not down there flicking her wings in butterfly netting."

"Oh, Mama, Mama," Tío Rico was crying again, only this time he was not playing any tango music. "Do you think they will hurt us?"

"Of course not, *nene*," Abuelita hummed, drawing Tío Rico to her scrawny breast.

My father got up and walked over to the banister.

"Excuse me, Your Excellencies, *Sirs*." My father bowed to the three judges. His white linen suit was beautifully pressed, the trouser pleats straight and the center as good as a plumb line. He looked, I thought, particularly elegant—one leg slightly in front of the other, the toe of his white suede shoe showing just a bit, his head cocked slightly to the right.

My father held the Panama hat that Tío Jaime had made for him in his hands. That hat was as wide as a chessboard.

"Gentlemen. Excellencies. Your most admirable Excellencies. It would seem to me and aaaahhh and uuuhmn, it would seem to me clear, and errr and ahh, absolutely that . . ."

Here my father stretched his chin up further into that practiced three-quarter pose that he would always assume for the camera, and continued, "It seems to me clear, no, indispensable, irresistible, completely absolutely logical that we . . ."

"Get to the point, will you?" shouted Oscar Vargas.

"That we," my father went on, looking peeved, "if we are indeed to be judged and tried, to be occluded, and assaulted and blamed and defamed in this uuhh, proceeding, in so far aahhh and eeerr and uhmn, we, the family, need and hereby with all due respect request a lawyer."

84

"A lawyer?" all three justices shouted at once. "A lawyer?"

"You mean, a dirty lying two-faced scum?" said the one. "A creature who swears and spits on two or three or four sides of any given question?" said the second. "A lizard who slithers and slimes his way through an issue?" said the third. "A lawyer?" they all yelled together, their mouths agape with collective revulsion.

"Well, yes," my father replied. "Exactly. A lawyer."

"Request denied," said Oscar Vargas. "No lawyers allowed."

"What?" said my father. "No lawyers allowed? See here, Vargas, this is highly irregular. That does not seem to me to be just."

"There is no justice on this earth. You know that. Not for any of us. Not a one of us comes with clean hands," interrupted Oscar Vargas.

"My hands," rejoined my father, "are clean."

"Indeed. That is the point. They are too clean."

"We are all innocent. And if we cannot avail

ourselves of a lawyer to represent us, what are we to do?"

"*Mala suerte*," said Oscar Vargas. "My job is to put you on trial, nothing more, nothing less."

My father was red in the face. I thought he might explode, then I thought that, instead, he was imploding. Certainly something appeared to be going off inside him.

"Soraida!" my father screamed. "We need Soraida. Release Doña Soraida at once, *ahora mismo*."

"Why should I?" said Oscar Vargas.

I could hear Soraida muttering under her breath, "Dirty sons of putrefacting whores, *pendejos*, milk-faced turds, *me cago sobre tu puta madre*."

"What about bail?" said my father.

"Now you're talking," said Oscar Vargas.

The three justices looked at one another. The spectators wriggled in their seats. Tío Jaime looked up from his chess manual. I thought he was about to say something but then he closed his mouth and started reading again.

"Now, Don Armando," asked Oscar Vargas. "What amount of bail are you proposing? For someone as important to you as you say this windbag of feathers is . . ."

"Watch it! Watch it!" Soraida screeched at the top of her parrot lungs. "Watch whom you call a windbag of feathers!"

"As I was saying," Oscar Vargas went on, ignoring her. "I would imagine you are prepared to post a substantial amount of bail for this personage, or, pardon me, parrotage."

"We believe Soraida should be released on her own recognizance," my father announced. "On her own word of honor."

"Now you are *not* talking," said Oscar Vargas. He rudely pointed to Soraida, still struggling to free herself. "Do you realize the seriousness, the gravity, of all this? Do you know what this spavined bassoon has been up to?" yelled Oscar Vargas melodramatically, pausing to take a sip from a thermos officiously offered him by one of the spectators.

"Treason. That is what. Subversion. Subversive activities: Disseminating. Anti-government propaganda. Electioneering. Casting aspersions. Calling the President of the Republic a cock-sucking whoremonger. I have a list of accusations against her three meters long!"

Soraida would be lucky if she were ever set free again, Oscar Vargas was saying. And if *he* had anything to do with it, she would be going away, upriver, to a correctional facility, *Adios*.

At this, Grita began crying again. Bracing herself against the banister, she chanted, "Soraida, Soraida," so loudly that even the alley cats under the tables took up her cry.

I looked in Grita's mouth and saw the encrusted backs of her six-year-old teeth. There were bits of cornmeal stuck on them, not to mention thin, fibrous cicada legs. I saw the silver fillings in her molars, her throat red and speckled. Her tongue was rattling wildly like a baby bird calling for its mother.

What a concert! I could see the spectators tapping time with their feet and nodding with their heads. "Hallelujah! Hallelujah!"

I heard the muffled *contrapunto* of Soraida's song—maggots, lizards, dog-faced liars, dirty sons of putrefacting whores. I heard the slam and bang of doors, the tumult of chickens in the kitchen, the whizzing of wings. It was a winding steam of songs, of blistering, boiling, heated melodies.

"Order! Order!" yelled Oscar Vargas. "Pull yourselves together." I could see that he had been much rattled by the confusion. He was wiping the eruption of sweat on his brow with a tea-stained rag and shading his eyes with the crook of his elbow.

"All right. All right," he said. "Now let me get this straight, Don Armando, you proffer no money for bail—you suggest instead that I release this blasphemous fowl on her own recognizance?"

"I do," said my father. "It seems only fair."

"And how is that?" said Oscar Vargas, taking a seat beside the three justices.

"Well," my father began. "We need Soraida to represent us, uhmm, to speak for us. That is since we are being denied a lawyer. None of us has any experience of the law with a capital 'L,' you see. We, it could be said, come from the school of no-knocks. And Soraida is the only one among us with the balls—that is, I mean, the knocks, the capacity, the talent—to speak— that is, to speak for each of us and all of us."

Tío Rico rolled his eyes and wagged his tongue. I do not know what he thought he was doing. Maybe he was just thirsty.

My mother sat in her chair, rocking, letting her eyes wander out the windows through the verandah, out to the cobblestoned street.

Oscar Vargas sighed. There were stains under his armpits and darts of perspiration on his shirt. Well, it *was* hot. He seemed to have lost some of his luster—why, his gold-edged teeth barely shone as he spoke.

"Since we are all under house arrest," my father interrupted, "what difference does it make if you let Soraida out of her prison to join us in *our* prison?"

Oscar Vargas looked tired. "The thing is to

get on with it," he said. Taking another swig from the thermos, he sank back into his seat. "If I release that damn parrot, the party will require a mega-generous contribution from you, Don Armando."

"Thank God!" exploded Soraida. "Not one more minute could I have endured that damnation of confinement. No creature should be made to stand the scratchy agony of hemp. My wings are raw; my skin is dry; you uncivilized gutter-born wretch. You can always tell the breeding of a man by how he treats a woman . . ."

"Careful, Jail Bird," cooed Oscar Vargas. "You would not want me to relent, would you? Put you back in a butterfly net, where certain up-pity parrots belong?"

Soraida looked at him with contempt but chose to exercise her right to remain silent.

CHAPTER TEN

A buelita repaired to her room. A white dust cloud escaped from the door as she slammed it tightly shut. She probably needed a nap.

The three justices had to fight their way through the crowd, past women with chickens sitting on their laps and pot-bellied boys sucking on candied sticks, to the corner where they had previously stashed a heap of cotton. I saw one of the children playing with the white stuff. One of the justices slapped the child's hand so sharply that you could hear the smack—and the ensuing howl—resounding from far away.

Each justice adjusted some of the cottony stuff on his head until rows of tiny white horsehair curls flopped like dog ears on either side of his face. If you looked hard, you could see where a machine had chainstitched the seams in the center of the identical parts.

Cheap goods, I thought.

Their wigs on, the justices placed black fabric around their shoulders and paused to admire themselves and one another. Whereas earlier, the three little men had looked to me to be an unimposing trio of *arepas*-and-cheese-eating loafers, the three now took on an aura of—I must admit it—magisterial authority.

And although Soraida frequently said, "Dress a monkey in gold and it is still a monkey," she might have been wrong in this instance. For surely these were three monkeys who were, if not dressed literally in gold, in their finery no longer still monkeys.

The bewigged and bedecked justices arranged themselves side by side at the table, while Oscar Vargas positioned himself in a most elaborate chair a few feet away.

It was difficult to distinguish the one justice from the other as they moved and spoke, it seemed to me, in concert, lifting their robes, adjusting their wigs, taking swigs of water out of paper cups.

Soraida had told me that one always had to appear to be in control. She told me that that was the secret of stage presence—to appear to be in control no matter how tired or frightened you might be—and she herself always took deep, measured breaths, filling her rib cage with air and counting one-two, one-two-three, before she performed, so to speak (or so *not* to speak, depending on the success of the performance).

"Ah-ha-ha-ha-he-ho-hum." Soraida was warming up in the wings. "Hum-ho-he-ha-h ha-ah." Rising and declining scales. "Mi-mi-mi-miiiii," she sang, moving her shoulders up and down as if slipping off a gown.

"Tell that parrot to clam up!" one of the justices shouted.

"Gag her—stuff a sock in her mouth!" yelled another.

Soraida ruffled every feather she had; she raised and whizzed her flapping wings, flicked her eyes yellow. But before she could say boo or

94

utter a peep, one of the justices said: "Let us now proceed."

This justice seemed to be more important than the other two, for he sat in the middle, just slightly raised above his brethren. We could see from where we now sat that they seemed to hold him in some deference.

Oscar Vargas banged a broom on the courtyard floor. He relaxed his mouth and sang in a tenor voice so clear you could feel his words course through your ears and veins and indeed ricocheting through your whole body.

"Oyez, oyez, oyez," the Magistrate chanted. Deeper and lower than any of the songs I had ever heard sung in that hot place. I heard it as the incantation of some dark night creature fighting for the light.

"Oyez, oyez, oyez. The Circuit Court is now in full session," Oscar Vargas intoned swaying from side to side.

"The Circuit Court is convened to hear the case of Romandía, family, Accused, and one Soraida Parrot, Defendants. All residents of Torre

Trece of this City of Aguas Calientes in the light of God and by the grace of His Excellency the President Plenipotentiary of the Republic and all of his and God's creatures."

The justices nodded gravely. One of them took out from under his black robe what appeared to be a rolled parchment the size of a baseball bat. It was tied with a satiny blue ribbon.

He then rose slowly from his seat, making sure that his black robe did not catch under the legs of the chair. He pulled off the ribbon and unrolled the parchment and, placing a pair of demilune spectacles on the tip of his long knobby nose, made a minor adjustment to the lurching wig on his head. Finally, he began to read from the document stretched out before him.

"Indictment Number 3,459.

"Whereas the said family of Romandía and the aforementioned Parrot, Soraida, have been accused of acts of sedition too numerous to mention.

"And whereas the said Parrot, Soraida, while under the control and exclusive dominion of the above-stated family Romandía, has been heard to disseminate propaganda of a sort to reach and dismay our most illustrious, beneficent President of the Republic, to have spread calumnies and defamations abroad and beyond by said Parrot's offensive manner of speech.

"And whereas the said Soraida, Parrot, has been a resident of and member of the family herein described:

"One. Grandmother, Abuelita, dusty, who wears chicken feathers on her eyelids.

"Two. Mother, Doña Clara, who rocks in her chair all day and sees beyond to what is—or what is not—there.

"Three. Father, Don Armando, impervious, so very particular, high-waver to women.

"Four. Jaime, fatuous manufacturer of felt hats that provide no shade and of pointed brassieres that make adequate cat bowls. A degenerate and a chess player.

"Five. Rico, incorrigible tango player, copious weeper, father to multifarious claimants.

"Six, Seven, and Eight. Two spoiled girls, one

reputedly a witch and the other simply a simp. And one Hortensia Salsipuedes, maid, devil-worshipper and olive-oil braider.

"And whereas the said Parrot, Soraida, has been a member of and participant in the goings-on of the afore-described Romandía family for generations, the issue is now joined and testimony will be entertained as to what, what indeed, and what precisely, what kind of a family would allow a parrot, a Guacamayo of the genus Psittaciformes, to say the kinds of things—to scream and yell or declaim and swear the kinds of things the accused parrot is now believed guilty of having said.

"What kind of a family is this?"

The Chief Justice sat back in his chair, wiped his brow with a frayed chicken-feather duster, opened up the tome in front of him and began flipping the pages the way Tío Jaime flipped the pages of his chess manual, not actually appearing to read or even see anything but flipping, flipping, flipping away nonetheless.

My father looked at my mother and then

glanced quickly at my Abuelita. My Abuelita looked at Tío Rico, and Tío Rico at Tío Jaime. Tío Jaime looked at Soraida, and my sister Grita and I looked at each other. The maid Hortensia Salsipuedes just looked superior.

Well, what kind of a family *were* we? Not one of us had an answer.

THE RUDE AWAKENING

No one had ever asked that question of our family before, at least not to our faces. Whether or not anyone had ever asked that question behind our backs, amongst themselves . . . well, leave it be.

It was a difficult question to ponder.

Tío Jaime picked up his chess manual. Hortensia Salsipuedes disappeared into the kitchen. My Abuelita swatted flies.

Soraida risked a glance at the Chief Justice focusing her clear eyes on the wavy white rivulets of his machine-made wig. She let out what sounded like a harrumph.

May I say here that one of Soraida's many talents was to let it be known exactly what she felt without having to utter a single word—and in this case I would argue that a harrumph is not a word. She could raise an eyebrow or shift her eyes and you knew exactly what she meant.

"Semiotics," Soraida once said. "Simple semiotics. The very essence of the stage—what is left unsaid."

Soraida's harrumph seemed to discomfit the Chief Justice for with both hands he proceeded to readjust his cheap wig.

"Well?" he bellowed. "What do you have to say for yourselves?"

From behind the gathering crowd my father stepped forward, still smelling of *pomada Verde de Rosas.* "Lunch. I mean it is er . . . uhm . . . time for lunch."

Various spectators nodded their heads in apparent agreement. As if responding to some inaudible signal, they riffled through the brown paper bags or the boxes or the *bolsas* or the *sacos* or whatever it was that they had brought with them into our midst. They pulled out long breads cut lengthwise and filled with thin slivers of meat or sausage, or cornmeal *hallacas* still string-wrapped in banana leaves and stuffed with stewed chicken and green olives. Some members of the audience set up makeshift griddles and broiled little steaks or rounds of floured fish. Others fried up slices of black-ripened *plátanos*.

It was starting to sound and smell like a restaurant in that courtyard, what with all the grilling and the spurting and the meaty smoke rising to our nostrils. "Pass the *aguacate*," someone yelled. "Give me some mango," yelled someone else. "I need more *arroz*," yelled another until it became intolerable for those of us who still had had no lunch and only a meager breakfast.

Besides, it was midday, it was boiling out—no time for business—everything was sizzling, scurrying, crawling, sliding sideways and front. It was too hot to think, too hot to be polite or to do anything else but drink *Guanabana* juice and take a nice long nap.

"Now, if you please," Oscar Vargas said looking askance at the munching crowd in the courtyard through his gold-rimmed sunglasses and peering with seeming distaste at one chewer after another. "If you please. Will the spectators please refrain from making spectacles of themselves. This is not a carnival!" He banged his fist on the table.

People started to chew more respectfully— that is, with their mouths closed for a change.

"Good," said Oscar Vargas. "That's better. Your attention, please. As the issue has now been joined, their excellencies the three justices, the Magistrate, the revered, admirable and just, will now proceed. Do the accused defendants, the Romandia family, and the accused defendant, Soraida, as agent and parrot of the accused family, have anything to say in response to the allegations leveled this day against them?"

"Absolutely we do," said Soraida. "Lunch. It is time for lunch. No one can be expected to think clearly without sustenance, most particularly me, with my low body mass. I feel faint. I need food."

The three justices stopped leafing through their books, and along with Oscar Vargas turned their respective heads in Soraida's direction.

There was applause among the spectators.

"Lunch," yelled my sister Grita, lurching vertiginously this way and that from the balcony.

"Order!" yelled Oscar Vargas, once again. "This is all too much! The point has been made." Ringing a large bell, he went on, "Hear ye, hear ye. The Traveling Circuit Court is now in recess. There will be a one-hour lunch break."

～o～

We all gathered for lunch, as we customarily did, around the table on the shaded porch overlooking the courtyard.

My father sat at the head of the table and fidgeted. "Now what?" he asked, letting his spoon splash into his bowl of chicken soup flavored with cilantro leaves.

"Eat," said Abuelita. "Eat your chicken *mijito*. And remember," she added, turning to my sister and me, "those who do not eat their chicken will get no dessert."

What dessert? I remember thinking. We never got dessert in that house. All we ever got was fruit, fresh fruit. Who was Abuelita trying to fool? We had already been accused of so many things that perhaps she did not want us to be accused of not having good desserts?

"Ayyyy, *mamita*," said my father, glancing at his soup bowl. "I'm so worried. You know these people. One minute they're your friends and the next, pfuish. *Adios*."

"Don't worry, my son," said Abuelita. "Eat first. Worry later. And besides," and here Abuelita paused to give import again to one of her favorite homilies, "no amount of worry ever paid the smallest debt."

"Doña Soraida," my father appealed, "surely you with your superior *inteligencia* can think of something!" And then he shlurped, rather loudly, some soup from the side of his spoon into his mouth.

Soraida was now fidgeting as well—not seeming to find a comfortable spot on her chair. She was eating mashed cornmeal with butter and cheese. She did not much care for chicken.

"What a question!" Soraida mused aloud.

"'What kind of family is this?' Who the God-damned hell knows?" Turning to me, she said, "Pass me the milk, dear. *Qué mierda. Pucha digo.* So what can we do?" she went on. "We must stall for time. Like the Vizier and his horse." (She was thinking, of course, of the tale from the *Thousand and One Nights*—those stories within stories without end or clear beginning which she told and retold before tucking us into bed. In return for one year of freedom, a condemned man promises to teach the Vizier's horse how to speak. In a year a lot of things can happen, he reasoned: the Vizier could die, the man himself could die, or, who knows, a horse could learn how to talk.)

"You must think of something," my father interrupted. "We certainly cannot think of anything ourselves. Or can we?"

Tío Jaime shook his head, "No," and went back to feeding his Galápagos turtle. My mother rocked in the chair and said, "Yes." (Was it, "Yes, we can think for ourselves," or "Yes, we cannot think for ourselves"?) Tío Rico was too busy to respond to my father's query one way or the other —too busy slicking back the brilliantine in his hair.

Abuelita nodded in every direction and said, "Whatever you say, *mijito*. Anything whatever." She motioned to Hortensia Salsipuedes to give my father more chicken soup.

"Hot, hot hot," demanded my father.

"*Rápido*," said Abuelita. "Make it snappy."

"*Si Dios quiere*," said Hortensia Salsipuedes, pulling out and kissing the cross she wore around her neck.

And of course we—that is, Grita and I— were never expected to answer any questions not directly addressed to us, which no questions ever were.

"So, that's that," said my father to Soraida, clasping his hands in front of his face. "Only you can save us now."

cannot see clearly anymore. It must be the chills curling my body.

I am warm, my neck is wet, my hair is mat-flat.

It is one of the effects of the fever—an inability to think in an orderly fashion. Have I gotten *any*thing right?

It was so complicated, so confusing.

Oh, to sleep again the way I used to! On those cool linen sheets smelling of starch, half-dozing in the blue dark made of those heated days when the sun is so bright that no curtain or slat-fronted shade, no iron-grill or filigreed gate could keep the light from seeping through.

Sleep is my tonic. I do not care if I dream as long as I sleep.

And I will sleep. Sleep and remember.

Soraida used to say that in sleep comes the answer. She told us that was what the Greeks believed. They slept in caves and waited for an oracle to answer their prayers in a dream. The Greeks, said Soraida, the ancient Greeks, not to be confused with the people there now, were "the seminal fluid of civilization," as opposed to, she explained, "just a fetid drop."

"If you lose your dream," Soraida often repeated to me, "you may as well lose your mind."

Well, in our family there seemed to be a great many dreamers and not all of them with a strong claim on their minds.

Of course, in those days I dreamed only of swimming in the cerulean waters of the *Caribe*, swimming and holding my bubbling breath underwater, sliding past salamanders and tadpoles.

We always went swimming at *Carnaval*. Down to La Guayra, passing the cracked earth cliffs and the flat plant fingers and the signs that looked like rusty bottle-tops: Orangina, Coca-Cola, round and down we went, past sulfurous vales where condors circled the sky until we could see the water, blue, between the cliffs.

We wore costumes at *Carnaval.* All week. Everywhere. Costumes made of tulle or cotton, beads and straw. Costumes we thought about the whole rest of the year, considering who to be— a Hawaiian princess? Little Red Riding Hood? Anything, really, so long as it meant wearing high heels and lipstick and maybe even a painted mouche on our cheeks.

Once the family all dressed up as Spanish dancers. My father and mother had costumes copied from a Goya painting. A long black mantilla and a flouncy polka-dot dress for my mother, and for my father a white bolero jacket trimmed in silver bells so that music could be heard coming off of him as he sauntered through the plaza. The plaza was only a few paces from our courtyard. Soraida said we could think of it as the courtyard of the city, what with the government houses all around and the cathedral that looked like our birthday cakes frosted all white and sprinkled with tiny silver beads.

Grita and I would skip down the street to the plaza dressed in our Flamenco dresses, holding fans and clicking our heels. First we would greet the statue of Simón Bolívar, *El Libertador.* Then Grita would feed the pigeons that lived in a birdhouse atop a column. She let them sit on her head and peck out the bugs and walk up and down her arms.

Soraida had warned us of the dictators that swaggered to the plaza from the gilt-domed Presidential Palace, *caudillos* with single names. Dictators so puissant that even when they were six feet under people feared they might still be alive somewhere, watching them and waiting to pounce.

She told us how General Gómez took all the drunks, liars, beggars and thieves he could find and put them on a raft. He had these derelicts towed upriver, and sunk with a blast of dynamite in the sludgy waters of the Orinoco where the piranhas could pick clean what was left of them.

It was in the plaza that the young men came to wave and wink at the Señoritas, but the Señoritas were cagey—they would spy on them through the slats of their verandah doors, smile behind their hands and point some of them out to each other.

Of course, that was in the days when people rode on horseback through the city and telephones did not exist, nor did any young lady worthy of that venerated name venture forth without the protection of a chaperone.

"Not the way it is now," said Soraida, with young women going to the movies with young men, all of them children really, sitting in the dark together. "Beware," she admonished. "Beware of the wandering hand."

Nothing could compare, Soraida sighed, to the time when a man would ride his horse right up to a woman's window—every day at the same hour—and tip his hat to her, saying not one word, not even daring to look into her eyes. "Most of my lovers," Soraida confessed, "were the silent type."

∽o∾

Let me say here that Soraida was never more impressive nor indeed more persuasive than she was on that trial day.

Many times beyond number Soraida had told me of the jitters an *artiste* suffers before striding onto a stage, gripped by the apprehension that something will go dreadfully wrong. But *une vrai artiste*, she maintained, is always able to convince herself that she is divine.

Soraida raised her beak high above her velvet head and at the same time puffed out her old-fashioned bosom (that oh-so-comforting bosom to which I had run again and again to lay my head and hear muffled through its downy softness the thuds of her stout parrot heart). When Soraida addressed the justices, it was with a voice so clear, so pure, and so true that I knew she must have believed herself at that very moment divine.

"Aaaoooooooiiiii," she sang out. Then, clearing her throat with a gesture that seemed to spring from her shoulders, she said, "Very well now."

"Very well now, what?" spat out one of the justices.

"Very well now, period. Let us begin, you dogdick."

An outcry arose in the courtyard—a tittering of voices punctuated by the kicking of hard heels and the shuffling of open-toed *alpargatas* on the tiles.

The Chief Justice clapped his hands and rose from his seat. "Order!" he said. "Order in the courtyard! We will tolerate no more outbursts of this raucous kind. Given the unusual nature of this case, we illustrious gentlemen of the law have decided that it is best to dispense with the usual Justinian rig-fa-rol. We will take a more Cromwellian common-law approach. We will entertain testimony and then weigh the evidence marshaled. What say you, Magistrate?"

"Excellent," replied Oscar Vargas. He turned

to Soraida. "Proceed, Madam. Tell us, what kind of a family is this?"

At the so harshly reiterated question, my father started. He clasped his hands before him and his expression darkened considerably. The bridge of my mother's nose twitched and her nostrils dilated. Tío Jaime flicked through the pages of his chess manual, fanning them like cards from a playing deck. Tío Rico pulled on the knot of his tie. My Abuelita stared straight ahead as if such a question had nothing whatsoever to do with her.

Again Soraida raised her beak, this time placing one foot in front of the other and resting her hand on a chair. "Dreamers, Your Honors— they are dreamers. But to dream is not a crime."

Oscar Vargas stood up. "Let *us* decide where a crime lies, my dear feathered lady," he said, picking up a ream of papers from the justices' table. "And you, my torch-singing beauty? You are no innocent, are you?" He waved a menacing forefinger in Soraida's face.

"You have been heard casting aspersions on His Excellency the President of the Republic, excoriating him as a whore-mongering, cock-dangling, turd-brained maggot on the cesspool of history. And, my future feather duster, repeating these calumnies not once but blowing them out of those windbag lungs of yours from these windows at all hours of the day, with this family of so-called dreamers fully awake and cognizant. How do you plead to that?

"Here," Oscar Vargas shuffled a sheaf of papers under Soraida's nose. "Here it says: Friday last, sometime before noon, the suspect yells '*Viva la liberté*, to hell with libertine Presidents and their *puta* whores.' And here, Wednesday, mid-month, mid-day: the suspect declares, 'Free yourselves! Say shit to your putrid jobs and piss on the yokes of your oppressors.' The list goes on and on. What, dear lady, do you call that? We call it anti-government propaganda, incitation to riot. We call it treason. What do you say to that?"

Soraida replied as cool as only she could be, "Artistic license."

"What?" said Oscar Vargas, incredulously.

"I said, artistic license."

"And whence did you obtain this license? And just who, may I ask, if not this family of reprobates, taught you to mouthe all those obscenities?"

It was here that Soraida let Oscar Vargas have a piece of her mind. Nothing infuriated her more than the notion that a parrot, any parrot, but most particularly she herself, mimicked human conversation, parroting such silly phrases, or as she would say, ludicrosities, as "Polly want a cracker?"

Oh, how Soraida bristled at such nonsense! To think of herself as merely a mimic! A mere pawn of a parrot! It was outrageous.

"Risible!" Soraida yelled at Oscar Vargas, streaking through the air from one perch to another.

"Preposterous!" she screamed. "Not to say invidious. Only my genius dictates to me what I say. It alone drives me. The genius I was hatched with, the genius that lives in the very marrow of my bones. Or should I say, in my very quills?"

At this last, Soraida inhaled deeply, flaring her nostrils before going on.

"What are you squawking about?" asked Oscar Vargas.

"Genius. I was born to use my gifts. To use them and reuse them. To talk. To sing, to rave, to whisper. To shout out loud. To spill forth noise divine. La, la, la, la, la. *Coloratura bravado soprano bellissima.* Cascading torrents, foaming white rivers of sound, gorgeous luscious irresistible sound, bucketsful of notes." Here Soraida took a deep singer's breath. "Genius. God-given."

The spectators stood up to applaud. The more sophisticated among them shouted, *"Brava! Brava!"* The less educated whistled or hooted. Everyone was affected—of that I am sure.

The applause must have been music, so to speak, to Soraida's ears, for she seemed only then to notice and enjoy the audience. She took a long bow, raising a wing and looking slowly from side to side.

Oscar Vargas was not amused. "Blasphemy!" he shouted. "What in the name of heaven do you, Madam, a mere scrawny bag of beaky thistle, know of what God gives or intends to provide? Answer me that, Madame Butterfly, or should I say Madame Butterfly *Net?*"

Soraida continued unperturbed and in full voice, "A very great deal more than you can imagine. Have you ever stopped to wonder why parrots fly?"

Soraida paused dramatically as if waiting for a reply. I could see one or two of the spectators nod their heads as if to say, "No, no never have."

"And by fly I do not mean in airplanes or pussmoths. We soar on our own, glide and loop. We fly to God for answers, that is why."

"What do you mean by answers?" interrupted Oscar Vargas. "I have been trying to get some around here and so far have gotten nothing but chicken fat."

"You are not asking the right question," Soraida explained. "I mean, have you ever stopped to wonder why some creatures never become anything more than eating machines?" Taking a sip of water, she went on, "The jungles of my birth were killing fields. Hatchlings torn from their mothers, feathers plucked from bodies, wings severed at the elbow. Plumes for fancy hats and signs of rank. Toucans, Guacamayos, loritos were all sacrificed to profane glory. Not to mention pet shops!

"I was born blind," she said, "so as to see. Featherless, so as to be many-plumed. A bony sack of loose flesh soon filled with the warmth of my mother's breath."

"Filled with hot air," said Oscar Vargas, "and I am certain, congenital bad breath."

Soraida merely glanced at him. "Every night I, a nursing babe waited, my head tenderly up-turned, rumpled from recent sleep, weaving from side to side, fear and hunger in my throat, waiting and hoping for that maternal silhouette to re-appear by the craggy entry of our humble moss-lined nest. There deep within a rotting tree, I trembled not knowing whether Mama too had been pulled apart for her beautiful feathers."

She had the audience in the palm of her claw; there was no doubting that. Onlookers began to weep. Someone blew his nose. I heard another one ask to borrow a tissue.

"How the jungles resonated with our cries and were bloodied sticky with the juice of our bodies," wailed Soraida.

"And so," she turned to Oscar Vargas, "to get back to your question, this family, these Romandias—womanizers, dancers, and dreamers though they surely be—are . . . are . . . "

"Full of shit!" bellowed Oscar Vargas.

CHAPTER THIRTEEN

Parrots are very clean—they minister to their bodies daily, pecking out the tiny larvae of moths from between their rainbow quills: It is a form of love-making. Soraida told me so.

Parrots prefer to travel in pairs. The pairs stay close, one flying right after the other to eat from the same branch and peer out at the same vistas, gliding together toward volcanic lakes. Flying together at night like shadows on a misted moon. Or so Soraida said.

"What about you?" Grita once dared to ask of Soraida. "You are all alone."

"I," she replied curtly, "am no fly-by-night parrot. I am divine. Though for years I had no name even," Soraida declaimed, spilling forth the full story of her life and ours to that tribunal,

125

"for centuries, in fact. Because, as you know, I have always been here. Seeing everything. Hearing all. But remaining unseen and unheard."

Just like we girls were meant to be.

Like Hortensia Salsipuedes who went along sloshing her pail? Or my mother who rocked in her chair all day, saying nothing?

Unseen.

Unheard.

I slid into rooms and hid behind doors. I opened drawers and sat in closets. I smelled old shoes and hugged old clothes. I buried my face in my mother's robes and sniffed for briny watery things.

"Madam," Oscar Vargas interrupted. "This is all very interesting, what you say about being nameless, etc., the circumstances of your birth, and so forth, but," and here he paused, "your story is not moving us forward in this matter. The matter we are here convened to address: the no small matter of treason.

"We are assembled here to hear the answer to what appears to be a simple question, and that question still remains unanswered. 'Just what, what kind of a family is this?'"

Soraida stopped to take a sip of water, raising one brightly manicured claw high in the air and draining the glass with great theatricality.

"If you have no ready answer to the question, perhaps the application of a little force might serve to refresh you?" Oscar Vargas blustered. "The pulling out of your tail feathers, perhaps, one by scruffy one? Or what about those tender downy plumes just under your dewy axilla? You won't be needing those anymore where you are going."

And with that, he stormed over to her and grabbed her by the shoulders.

"Get your hands off me, you dirty filthy masturbating little worm!" Soraida sputtered, trying to claw him. "Unhand me, peanut dick!" She shook free of him and extended her wings.

"What kind of a tribunal does not allow one to seek the truth?" she asked. "And the truth cannot be stated in a sentence, What kind of a family is it, you ask—just like that. Do you think families spring up like random seedlings or smarmy pods? No," she said in answer to her own question. "Indeed not. Families are like jungles. They take time—generations, centuries, millennia. And every once in a while one needs a machete to clear the undergrowth, to get rid of the weeds and the chokers."

There was a ripple among the spectators. It was getting hard for me to hear anything, there was so much murmuring and sussuring. It was as if they had nothing better to do all day than sit around and listen to other people's problems.

Soraida remained unruffled. "If I could be permitted to continue without officious interruption," she implored.

"The Romandías are simple folk," she went on. "Simple people with simple tastes. Abuelita is drawn to dining room chairs, for example. What could be simpler than that?"

And so Soraida kept going, telling the justices most of our dearly husbanded family stories, extolling the deeds—the *hazañas*—of our immediate family and those of our forebears, those musty phantasms that Soraida maintained still crowded around the dining table, slapping their thighs and smiling their toothless pink smiles, waiting their turn to tell a tale.

In the course of Soraida's meandering recitation, a trio of students with bright multi-colored streamers hanging from their cloaks strolled into the courtyard. They began to strum their guitars and sing, ambling from one cluster of spectators to another, discreetly passing a soft hat among the assembled, who, weary perhaps from all the legal discussions were all too glad to give the three a *locha* or two and to encourage the youths with their tunes.

When the trio started playing a tango, Tío Rico must have found it irresistible, for down the banister he slid and, before she could demur, grabbed Soraida firmly about the waist. He led her dipping and deep-knee-walking about the courtyard, with great palm-slapping to and fro of his knees, front kicks between her legs and back slides, looking over his shoulder this way and that, the musicians playing along to his dance. Tío Rico bent Soraida all the way back over his knee. She pointed a leg in the air; he pulled her up; she stretched a wing.

"*Qué bonita eres*, Soraida, Soraida!" A cry rang out from the audience which was now on its feet, clapping along. "Encore, encore! Sing us a song," someone yelled. "*Cielito Lindo*." Another voice shouted, "*Fumando Espero*."

But Oscar Vargas put a stop to that. "Please!" he said. "Order. This is not a variety show. You," he signaled out Tío Rico. "Sit down. No more dancing! You," he addressed the musicians, "get out. And you," he eyed Soraida. "No singing!"

He said he wanted to hear Soraida talk not sing. "The family," he said. "You were telling us all about the Romandías."

Soraida had no *remedio* but to catch her breath and keep on talking.

She told about Arawaks and Caribes, mostly river paddlers ruled by *Caciques* with fierce names like Guaicaypuro or Tamanaco or Naiguata. She told about *Caciques* who fought the Spaniards and were torn limb from limb by savage dogs. Soraida's stories were so vivid. I could visualize the human meat, still stringy, caught between the dog's bloodied incisors.

It was then, said Soraida, that the Romandía family crest became a bleeding hand.

"What?" said Oscar Vargas.

"Crests, after all," Soraida admonished all of us, "must have something to do with the history of the families they front."

"Well, go on," said Oscar Vargas.

Our great-great-grandfather Ismael had a wife named Rosa, said Soraida. They were among the first settlers of the country. The land was far from tame. All around were cannibals who saw in the white man a good protein supplement— before you knew it, you could be gumbo.

So that when three fearsome warriors crept headfirst into the house of our great Romandía progenitor, Doña Rosa knew what was likely to happen to her—meat and bones for soup—and she knew, too, what had to be done. She flung herself furiously at the intruders. With all her strength, she tried to prevent them from reaching her husband by raising her hand.

"Whooo-aaack!" said Soraida, going on to explain that Doña Rosa's hand was summarily hacked off at the wrist.

"Whooo-aaack," Soraida repeated with, it seemed to me, slightly unbecoming enthusiasm.

The hand, still pulsing, still bleeding, was lowered into the ground holding a lily to rest atop our great-great grandfather who lamentably met his end in front of Doña Rosa, her sacrifice notwithstanding.

"So you see, señor," said Soraida to Oscar Vargas, "it was no picnic."

Soraida had told us that everyone as far as the eye could see was descended from one Indian or another—some Aztec princess or Inca chieftain. And, it goes without saying, from the European kings, too. She would take us to see their portraits in the *Galería Nacional*: the Spanish *Reyes* with their beefy lips and the Portuguese sovereigns with their hang-dog faces.

"What a voyage they undertook," Soraida exclaimed to those assembled. "It was what you might call a trip to hell, sailing on leaking galleons that rollicked on the vast steely-cold seas week after week. Food rotted, bodies scurvied, rats scurried. And then, once arrived on this continent, what did they find but heat and sickness and slithery creatures.

"And then the Viceroys came. And the Regents, pock-marked from measles. They were men pining for lost youth and missed kisses, longing for miracles in the mountain lakes. Expedition followed expedition, each one searching hopelessly for an El Dorado brimming with golden waters and banked by emerald shores.

"Men," said Soraida, "men are all the same. Only men could be foolish enough to believe in all those fairy tales. Women have far too much sense. They at least look for the fountain of youth in a jar that they can keep safely at home on top of their night tables."

Oh yes, many men came. They came from all over the world, not just from Moorish Spain and

Portugal. There were English seamen, younger brothers with no patrimony. Germans. Chinamen. Israelites. Men who left their women behind. "And why not?" said Soraida. "Here they found lovely Incas and charming Guaranís chewing curare to fecund their lust."

At that, my Abuelita clapped her hands over my ears. Lust, she felt, was not a fit subject for children, but Soraida was of a different persuasion—she wanted to feed everything into our brains before they became spongy and steamed in brown butter—which as we knew never kept well in the tropics.

"Some women came, too," added Soraida, "too tenacious to be left in the Old World where everything that was ever going to be known was known. And besides, here there were bougainvillea growing in the courtyards and breezes whispering of love.

"Love," Soraida went on to tell the justices, "is the sweetest of pleasures but available to a chosen few." And then, sonorously, Soraida went on to speak of herself. "For who among you," she demanded, "has flown high above ochre roof tops, soared on the wings of a strong and reckless mate, rested your head on his fanning tail feathers and glided in the vacuum of his wake?"

I can only now imagine, as I lie in these sweat-soaked linens, Soraida making love. I see two parrots flying together, Soraida dilating her cloacal bud for some even more magnificent creature to enter her. Or so I imagine. For what could I possibly know of intimate parrot things?

Suddenly it started to rain—huge, hurtful pellets plummeting into the courtyard and onto all the spectators and the three justices and Oscar Vargas and Soraida. People fought to get under cover, their big toes and soles soaked through their nubby canvas *alpargatas*. They stood under the big gnarled tree whose leathery leaves could now at last thirstily drink, stood while the salamanders and waterbugs rode the fast-moving rivulets into the drains.

And there was Soraida, with her tail spread, and her wings open to the rain, letting it soak every-which-way into her raised feathers. She seemed so happy as she began snapping at the raindrops with her ewer-shaped beak.

We heard thunder. Loud but from a distance. I thought of the gods with their mammoth marching drums careening cantankerously through the slate-grey skies.

"Water recess," gargled Oscar Vargas. "Recess."

CHAPTER FOURTEEN

Soraida used to say it was a lucky thing that she could see better than most other of God's creatures. It was her eyes: they had no whites, no room for sliding, no room to slip.

They were always zooming in every direction, forward and backward and to the side—she could tell what someone was doing behind her back as well as what someone thought he might be doing in front of her.

She never did trust Hortensia Salsipuedes. Soraida had the feeling, she told me, that Hortensia Salsipuedes was out to get her for some reason, something to do with her *brujerías*, those silly superstitious notions of Hortensia Salsipuedes's that came into that head full of shredded papers and dusty rags.

Soraida said that everything reduced down to talent. Hortensia Salsipuedes's gift she maintained was for cleaning—sloshing that sudsy pail of hers, making those beds and sorting those clothes—and in any case not for thinking. And when persons get confused and lose track of where their talents lie, they get, shall we see, derailed.

It was a good thing, it seemed to me, that Hortensia Salsipuedes was a talented cleaner. We Romandías were a messy lot. Soraida always said so. "Messy, messy, messy." And believe me, it takes a parrot to know.

Tío Jaime left chess men all over the house: games half-played and half-won, black pawns and white pawns. There was little to be done about the chess men in the linen closet, in between the sheets or in the kitchen with the chickens and there were always one or two chess men sunk at the bottom of Hortensia Salsipuedes's pail. And all those pointy brassieres lined up on the dining room table. "Well," said Soraida, "at least the *pobrecito* tries to do something, poor mama's darling, not like that Tío Rico of yours."

But it seemed to me that Tío Rico was always busy, what with his *bandoleón* playing and his tango lessons. Not to speak of all those putative children of his.

Abuelita doused them, each and every one, with dust. She kept her dust in a tin on her tulle-skirted dresser, dusting anyone who even brushed by her. With so much dust about, it did not surprise me that Hortensia Salsipuedes had really nothing so very nice to say about any of us. Or, for that matter, about Soraida who was always scolding her about leaving dirt balls in corners. What *would* surprise me was how *many* things—none of them good—Hortensia Salsipuedes had to say about us when she was called on to testify.

"This tribunal is now in session," Oscar Vargas said. "We call to the stand one Hortensia Salsipuedes, unindentured servant and *idiote savante.*" At this my father straightened and glanced at my Abuelita as if to ask, Why her?

Oscar Vargas made Hortensia Salsipuedes swear on a Bible that everything she was about to say was true.

"So help me gods," said Hortensia Salsipuedes rolling her eyes upward—presumably to heaven.

Then at Oscar Vargas's prompting Hortensia Salsipuedes sat down in one of the wooden chairs and began to describe her years of employment and enumerate her duties, interrupting herself with many "if the gods will it," "gods bless," and so forth.

"Tell us," asked Oscar Vargas, "how came you here before us?"

It was there and then that Hortensia Salsipuedes admitted, "It was me who denounced Soraida to the police. I just could not listen to that demon-hag of feathers screeching anymore —maybe now I can finally get some rest. For years I have had to plug my ears with cold tea bags to keep from hearing that old trollop."

"Who are you calling a trollop, you suppurating old witch? You who have betrayed us?"

screamed Soraida, trying to claw at Hortensia Salsipuedes. "Nothing ever filtered in at all through those sticky cobwebs you call brains," added Soraida. "You piece of . . ."

Oscar Vargas tackled Soraida. "Quiet down now, before I have you restrained. This is a court of law. Go on please, Señorita Salsipuedes. It is Señorita, is it not?"

"It is," said Hortensia Salsipuedes.

"Only technically, you old *puta*," said Soraida. "None of them would ever marry you."

Hortensia Salsipuedes slicked back her olive-oiled hair with the palm of one hand and stretched her one good dress over her bony knee with the other. "That bird thinks I am blind and deaf to all their squabbles, but I am not. I know . . . I know *everything*. They don't wipe their behinds. They throw their smeared underwear on the floor and expect me to pick it up."

I held my hands to my ears.

"They pick their noses and scrape the boogers on the walls!" said Hortensia Salsipuedes.

That was a horrible thing for Hortensia Salsipuedes to blurt out to strangers. But not as horrible as what she was saying, now, calling Grita a witch-child who gnawed on lizards and licked squeezed cockroaches between her fingers.

"That one," she said, pointing at Grita, "with the mangled hair standing straight up. She hacks the heads off chickens with a meat cleaver and says she's playing 'Doctor.' *Witch* doctor!" screamed Hortensia Salsipuedes, still pointing at Grita.

"*You* are the witch *de mierda*," screeched Soraida. "Voodoo-worshipper."

"All they eat is chicken," howled Hortensia Salsipuedes. "Boiled, steamed, dunked chicken. Shredded, chopped, diced chicken. Chicken fried. Chicken stirred. Chicken eggs and chicken soup. Chicken with beans and chicken with rice. Chicken with potatoes. Chicken casserole and chicken *portugaise*. Chicken cutlets and chicken patties. Chicken, chicken, chicken. I am sick of chicken."

"*You* make *me* sick," said Soraida, "and you're no chicken. Go eat your own mother."

"May all the bats in hell drop turds on your mother's grave!" yelled Hortensia Salsipuedes.

"Ladies, ladies," Oscar Vargas intervened. "This is not a *mercado libre*. Let us have some decorum. Now Señorita Salsipuedes, can you enlighten us, without undue emotionality, as to what kind of a family is this."

"They do not believe," said Hortensia Salsipuedes drawing herself taller in her seat. "They do not believe in anything."

"How is that, Señorita Salsipuedes?" asked Oscar Vargas.

"They have no religion." She crossed herself and kissed her thumb. "They never even go to church. They know nothing of the saints and the Cross or the Holy Ghost, may He rest in peace."

"Anything else, Señorita Salsipuedes?" asked Oscar Vargas.

"The cats!" she volunteered. "They are so mangy that even the fleas on them have nowhere to hide. But the way the old lady protects them you would think they were her children and probably they are more rewarding than those three good-for-nothing sons of hers."

My father was staring at Hortensia Salsipuedes very, very sternly. I could tell that he would never give Hortensia Salsipuedes a raise after that last locution.

"Worse than nothing, complete riffraff," she added.

"My good woman," blurted out my father. "You are abusing not only us but yourself."

Hortensia Salsipuedes went on nevertheless. "And by riffraff I mean the one who plays chess all day and grows hats in a factory like so many banana leaves, and the other one who is so busy chasing women that he has forgotten how to count just how many children he has sired by now. And as for the girls' father, Don Armando, now there's a *parrandero*. He went and tasted all the wild things he could find, gad-hopping about the world like a slick-tongued lizard after flies. He brought home a bride young enough not to know about men like him. Now all Doña Clara can do is rock in a chair."

You can imagine the effect of this diatribe on my poor father. If he never appreciated being compared to his brothers, still less did he like any reference being made to his age, even less did he like anyone speaking of my mother in any but the most reverential of tones.

When my father stood up I noticed that his white linen suit looked a little wrinkled at the knees and upper leg, but his blue tie with the embroidered bees was still impeccable. Quite red in the face, he turned to Hortensia Salsipuedes: "You whom we took in have taken us in! You whom we have practically raised as a member of this family! Cease and desist in your calumny. Or get the hell out of my house!"

"'Avaunt and quit my sight,'" Soraida piped up.

"I will not," said Hortensia Salsipuedes.

"Pack up your *peroles*. You are fired," said my father.

"You cannot fire me," said Hortensia Salsipuedes. "I have immunity."

It was, I knew, more than distressing for my

145

father to realize that Hortensia Salsipuedes had nothing really kind to impart about him, or any of the rest of us. But as Soraida used to say, "Disappointment is the coriander of life: you do not always know what it is but you can always taste it."

CHAPTER FIFTEEN

We never missed our *merienda*. No matter what, come mid-afternoon we would all gather ravenously around the table in anticipation of something delectable to fortify us and keep us good-humored until dinner. And nothing, not even the trial, not even Hortensia Salsipuedes's abominable *diabluras* could keep us from our daily ritual.

Soon the kettle on the old stove in the kitchen was whistling its grating tune, and Hortensia Salsipuedes was shuffling her slippered feet back and forth to the table. A platter of toasted bread rounds appeared, followed by a larger one containing sliced chicken. My father was staring at Hortensia Salsipuedes with what can best be described as homicidal fury, and who could blame him?

Still, it was hard for me to hate Hortensia Salsipuedes. She had betrayed us, it is true, but I was a child, I did not realize then what that betrayal meant. For years, not a day went by in that house when someone did not tell Hortensia Salsipuedes to pack her *peroles* that instant, but never did she leave for more than an afternoon. And these eternal firings became part of our life in that place. Whether or not she would survive to live another day in our midst I did not know— my father was still glaring at her.

"She is just a poor ignorant woman," my Abuelita said, dismissing Hortensia Salsipuedes as if she were not present.

"A conniving superstitious fusspot," sputtered Soraida.

"A truly horrible person," said my father trembling as he reached for the guava paste and cream cheese. "The worst."

"God forgive them," said Hortensia Salsipuedes, looking once again heavenward, "for they know not what they do."

"We do know what we do," snapped my mother, rocking vacantly back and forth.

"You are the mother of a witch," replied Hortensia Salsipuedes, jutting her knobby chin out at Grita who was chewing with her mouth wide open and pushing what spilled out of it back into it with her index finger.

"Stop that Grita," said Soraida sharply. "When have you ever behaved so disgustingly?"

"All my life," Grita answered back, spitting with her mouth still full.

"You should know your manners better than that," said Soraida, "and leave your kitchen manners where they belong!"

We girls had spent a great deal of time following Hortensia Salsipuedes about the house and kitchen. And if Hortensia Salsipuedes really did leave, then what would become of us? We had Soraida, but Hortensia Salsipuedes was also instructive.

149

There was always so much to see and do in the kitchen. It was the largest room in the house, with a big skylight and pots always steaming on the stove, doughs rising in their towel-covered bowls, coffee tins jammed with chicken feathers.

Most mornings, we greeted the chickens in their cages and watched as their fluffy down floated into the light. The cages were covered with a gummy stuff which Grita liked to chew— with her mouth open, of course. She said that it tasted better than candy, better than gum, and certainly better than chicken.

"Anything tastes better than chicken," Hortensia Salsipuedes would say as she poured herself a glass of *chicha*. She made *chicha* from oatmeal which she chewed and spat out and let stew for days or even weeks in a pail under the sink.

Chicha seemed to make Hortensia Salsipuedes voluble, if not positively garrulous. Sometimes, when Grita and I were in the kitchen, in between sips of *chicha* she would tell us about her former husband or, as she was careful to say, "the father of my children." He was some sort of soldier—a police officer. I think he was. His occupation did not seem to matter much. It was his *pre*occupation that interested Hortensia Salsipuedes. Hortensia Salsipuedes's husband liked to consort with low women. "*Putas,*" she elucidated. "Men," she pronounced, "are made for sin."

Hortensia Salsipuedes pulled a picture out from somewhere under her dress to show us. It had been folded over so many times it looked like the pieces of skin we peeled off our arms when the sun burnt them too red.

"Men," she hissed. "They will have their way with you and then spit you out like yesterday's *chicha.* They will hold your hand and then they will want to hold and to have the rest of you. And before you can say stop, stop, they will be pulling their filthy wretched things out. . . ."

∽∘∽

"Enough," we heard Oscar Vargas shouting. "Let's get on with the trial. Have you had enough time to perfume yourself, you smelly old bird?" he snidely inquired.

"I do not use scent," Soraida answered matter-of-factly. "Perfume is nothing but the foamed spittle of so many mosquitoes sizzling on so many tree trunks. Clearly, a substance meant to rouse a male hornet to copulation is not meant to be on my body."

"Then if you are ready, please do go on, Doña Soraida," said Oscar Vargas. "Fill in some of the gaps left by the previous testimony."

Soraida took a deep breath, then launched into one of her favorite tales.

How the original Romandía first marched onto these shores, infested with crawlers and fern-tongued lizards that licked up their sweat and tickled their toes—how he rode down the gang-plank on a sweat-shiny horse that was rearing and bucking and all decked out in silver squash blossoms.

Did you know that in the same year that Christopher Columbus sailed for the glory of *Isabel la Católica* to these very Americas the Spaniards expelled their Jews? They in turn fled to the New World, but even here, in this land covered with vines and burgeoning trees, there was no place to hide. The Spaniards exported their inquisition.

"Just as you are doing now," Soraida cried out to the justices, "searching and sniffing like dogs for clues that lie in embers in some rusty plant tin."

Soraida said so many things to us that trying day, teaching, nudging. "Making you see," she said. "Making you see."

Soraida told the judges of a mythological zoo that once upon a time, she swore, really did exist. A zoo of human dwarfs, green-eyed pumas, and birds whose iridescent plumage was more resplendent than the sun, more lustral than the moon. Warriors brought back these trophies from the Southernmost reaches where the hills were scalp-headed and frigid and the rivers looked like liquid silver. And from the North where it was colder still and men wore down on their ocher-stained bodies. From all the corners of all the kingdoms came these never-before-or-since-seen creatures.

The runners who discovered them had

waxen-black hair and chewed manioc. They prayed to a serpent born of breath.

Yet in the end the jungle grew over everything, consuming their very footsteps, choking the cities with hanging vines.

And the zoo? The zoo went up in flames. "I was in that zoo," Soraida confessed, starting to cry. "After the fire, I dragged my singed wings on the ground."

All she could do, she elaborated, was eat the fruit that had splattered on the ground, the stub-fingered hands of bananas, the wet stringy mangoes.

"I made my way past butterflies the size of rabbits, past winged dragons," Soraida said. "It was here that I came. This land on the other side of the fires and the sickness. Safety and sanctuary."

∽○∽

I see my own face staring back at me, but from where? It must be the fever which is broiling up my body and frying in my brain.

"Oh, for a cup of lapsang souchong tea, that

scent of musk and smoke; for toasted ham and cheese sandwiches piled high on a plate and tangos playing at three."

Who is speaking?

My chest oppresses me. I cannot breathe. Yet still I can remember—that is my destiny. I hear my mother telling the justices just who she was. At first she made sense and then she did not.

"I do not belong here," she told Oscar Vargas. "In this world of so strange creatures with their fetid mouths and strangled breaths. I come from the South, where the seasons change and the cities are proper cities not dust-covered ruts. And a pastry is something sweet, made with real butter, and not some hybrid of bird and insect droppings. Here everything shines, shines like a vulgar new coin."

Funny, Soraida used to say, how everyone wants to shine: gold chains, gold rings, gold teeth.

"I belong in other places, with other people. I am not of here." I was not sure she was *even* here—it was my mother talking.

155

I imagine it may take me time to understand. I have no one to teach me, to make things simple.

I can hear the rocking of my mother's chair. One foot up and one foot down.

"I do not know what made me think that I could ever understand the ways of this place."

"And just why is that?" asked the Magistrate.

"Because I am from the Río de la Plata, the low flat pampas. I was brought here when I was very young, a child really myself."

"So what is it that you do not understand?" asked Oscar Vargas.

"My mother-in-law wears false eyelashes made out of chicken-feathers, need I say more?" she replied. "She eats her vegetables off a knife."

"That is all very well—get to the quick of the thing: What kind of a family is this?"

"I am not sure that I can say," she said. "You know, I am much younger."

"How so, Madam?"

"Much younger than my husband."

"And how is that relevant?"

"And I have heart palpitations."

"Rather unusual in one of your stated youth, is it not?"

"Not if you knew all I have suffered," said my mother.

"Pray continue," said Oscar Vargas.

"The maid is off on Sundays. I have to get down on my knees, the place is such a mess. I scrub between the tiles, I do!

"And Armando," my mother continued, "is out all day, every day—wherever it is he goes, because you know he is certainly not in trade. No one in our family is in trade, except for Jaime, of course, but then my dear brother-in-law Jaime has never netted a *centavo* out of that hat factory of his."

"And why is that, Doña Clara?" Oscar Vargas asked.

"Quite simply, because no one of sound mind buys heavy felt Homburgs in the tropics." At this my mother paused and looked meaningfully at my father and then at Tío Jaime.

That was all my mother talking. But she

usually did so little talking, how did she manage to do so much that day?

"Jaime has littered the country with that ever-expanding line of felt bowlers, and now it threatens to extend from mountain to sea. Why bowlers can now be found on the remotest of beaches—and the turtles have to be careful not to mistake them for other turtles.

"And now," my mother continued. "Jaime is going to also make brassieres. And Armando approves. The brassieres Armando wants Jaime to manufacture look like pairs of cardboard dunce caps with pointed spiral cups and tips like metal spikes. No woman in her right mind is going to buy a pointed brassiere that is as hard as the skin of an avocado."

"Very interesting, Madam, fascinating in fact, but not very enlightening if you do not mind my saying so," interrupted Oscar Vargas.

"I promise to love this city of Aguas Calientes when—and not until—it has properly paved streets, not *barrancos* of mud, and restaurants with white table cloths and people who wear leather shoes. I will love it, Aguas Calientes, when it is completed. Right now it is a work-in-progress."

"Doña Clara Romandía," said Oscar Vargas, "I'll have you know that I am personally responsible for the re-beautification of these streets you call *barrancos* of mud and I take it as a personal affront that you find this city less enchanting than your native country, and where by the way did you say that was?"

"Argentina," said my mother.

"Argentina?" said Oscar Vargas. "That explains it. The land of pomaded sissy-men? Here we have real *liki-liki* dressed *machos*. Perhaps that is what you do not understand, *el macho criollo?*" At this he shot a glance at my father. "No wonder you are all so confused. Don Armando lusted after a yummy la-di-dah from the silvery South and then stupidly made her his wife. You may step down, Madam."

III

THE DIMINUENDOING

O kay, last chance," howled Oscar Vargas. "What kind of a family is this? Give me a reason not to hang you all!"

"They laughed at my jokes and applauded my songs," said Soraida. "Then, there is Abuelita," said Soraida, pointing out my grandmother. "See for yourself—dust unto dust."

At this all the spectators turned to look at my Abuelita, with as much alarm as wonder— no doubt wondering just how much dustier she could get.

"And then," said Soraida, "there is Jaime." Again the spectators shifted their gaze toward my uncle. "He has the business acumen reserved only to children and prelates.

"And then of course," said Soraida, "there is

Rico, whose main interest is—well, you can see for yourself, as many of his children are here in this courtyard." At this Tío Rico's children shot up, one by one, and did a flashing dance before sitting down again. I must confess they looked very nice, all neatly dressed and curled.

"And Don Armando and Doña Clara," Soraida went on, "and their two little girls, the flowers of the family." Here Grita lurched onto the balcony railing and hung by a hooked foothold so all the world could see her bloomers beneath her dress.

"Big deal! A bouquet of madhouse flowers!" pronounced Oscar Vargas.

"They descend from Don Able de Santa Lucia, Don Able Romandía de Santa Lucia y Gracia great-great-grandfather of the *familia* in question. He is where it began," said Soraida. "With Able. Able who left his brothers and quite possibly a bride, back in Saint Jean de Luz and sailed across the bounding main."

"What on earth was he looking for?" barked Oscar Vargas.

"What all men on earth desire," replied Soraida. "He had to leave Europe to find it."

Here, Soraida continued, Able found land aplenty in the great pampas and *sabanas*, where all you could see were the swamp grasses and herons and mud hills. Able bred sheep, bred cattle, grew coffee.

At night in his bed in the dark dankness of the hours he dreamed of the boulevards and horse-drawn carriages of the world he left behind.

But here in these far different climes he heard birds sing, and he never felt cold.

With so many colors and sounds, it did not take long for Don Able to stop dreaming of what he had left. All around him the young man saw full forgiving lushness—charming *meztizas* and lovely *criollas*, burgeoning bulbs in these sulfurous parts. He saw cinnamon women in the open-air market selling maize and hand-loomed fabrics and birds of every description.

"So!" interjected Oscar Vargas. "It was women he came for!"

"I am referring not to women," said Soraida, "but to birds—birds, if you will, of a feather."

"Get on with it then!"

The birds came from the *sabanas* and the *selvas* where their plumage was camouflaged by the multi-colored leaves. All you could see of them was perhaps an eye here, the flash of a beak there—and that was only if you were concentrating, for you could unseeingly pass the odd *lorito* or toucan.

Don Able would go alone and unheralded to the Square on those market mornings. He would cock his ears to the tunes of macaws and *loros*, all of them singing at once. It reminded him of the Basque country whence he had come. Or of the phantom girl he had perhaps deserted.

Soraida was telling how Don Able had seen her and taken a fancy to her. "He recognized my fine talents. Under my tutelage his lands bore fruit and his house prospered and the Romandías took hold in Aguas Calientes. And I am here to assure you it was no toehold. Don Able had seen in a dream that he should sail forth."

166

"Who cares?" said Oscar Vargas. "My patience is running out. You, worm bag of a bird, have presumed to call the President of the Republic a cocksucking, motherfucking murderer, and where did you get these ideas if not from these Romandías? Where does a *carajo pinche* parrot like yourself get the gall to rattle on about Don Able?" As Soraida would have put it, the hairs on his tongue were running amok. "*What kind of a family is this, anyway?*"

"It is a family of dreamers," replied Soraida. "Dreamers all. Nothing more than dreamers. But nothing less."

CHAPTER SEVENTEEN

Funny how the wind stops just before it is about to rain. How everything stops. No one dares to walk. Or to crawl. Even talking slows. Even swallowing. Even breathing. Only sweating comes naturally.

The cicadas start twanging their guitar tunes, the toucans creak like rusty swings. And I sing too—no, I do not sing, I cry out. I cry out at night, alone in this heat. I cry out for Soraida.

First you hear the thunder. And then you feel the rain.

Oh it was so hard to go on, seeing people eating with their mouths open or scratching at their privates, attending to their business as if nothing was happening to us, Romandías.

Oscar Vargas was saying something. Nothing of great interest I thought at the time. But what did I know then? Or, come to think of it, now?

"No one but dreamers could have borne the waters, the *zancudos*, the mutinies and treasons," said Soraida. "Grandfathers killed, mothers dying in childbirth, uncles devoured by jackals. This land was treacherous—it was inhospitable. First the seas swallowed the beaches and belched forth tidal waves as high as mountains. And then the *temblores* came thundering and slashing and gnawing at the earth itself."

"Don't forget about the snakes," wailed Grita. She meant the anacondas that Soraida had told us about—they lived in low branches over the river, ready to pounce not only on naughty little girls but on baby parrots, which they preferred to eat whole. Letting them dissolve in their stomach juices over several days.

"Only dreamers," Soraida was telling Oscar Vargas, "would embark on such a voyage. Can't you see," she implored, "the Romandías are not bad people. There is no reason to try them."

Oscar Vargas said, "High Treason is reason enough."

"Says who?"

"Say we, we the State. We his Excellency the Plenipotentiary Most Beneficent President of this Republic. We, his loyal lieutenants. And we have had just about enough from you, my feathered hag."

Oscar Vargas was leaning back, licking his cigar and balancing himself on the chair's hind legs. I prayed and waited for God to strike him down, even as I noted that Soraida never let *us* lean back that way. We were made to sit up straight with our hands in our laps—*or else*. Suddenly, Oscar Vargas sprang forward.

"High Treason carries the penalty of death," he said. "A slow, painful death."

Soraida gasped. My father began to stammer, "But, but . . . er . . . hmnnn. Just a minute here."

"So far," Oscar Vargas went on, "I have heard not a single good reason not to hang all of you. In fact," he went on, picking at something between

170

his teeth, "your obliteration would seem to me to be a very positive thing for Aguas Calientes."

I sat there, daring to hope that one spectator, just one member of that motley audience would leap up and object, denounce that remark for the outrage it was to the most illustrious family in Aguas Calientes. But not one person there in that courtyard moved. From the spectators all we heard was wheezing though stuffed-up nasal passages.

"Barbarian!" shouted Soraida. "You try innocent people for their dreams, and you dare to suggest *death*!"

"Enough!" cried Oscar Vargas. "We know less now than when we began!"

"The point," said Soraida, "the whole magnificent point is that knowing is irrelevant. The world is one long uninterrupted dream. God's dream. All the gods that ever were. Even you have heard of Vishnu, I trust?"

"Vishnu, snish-nu," replied Oscar Vargas. "You think this is a joke? A dream. It is in fact all too real." He grabbed her by the scruff of her neck. "Prepare to meet your maker. You have to account for yourselves!"

"For what?" said Grita. "I'm a good girl. I haven't done a thing. It wasn't me. *She* did it," she slapped at me. "She tried to strangle me."

"She started it," I yelled.

"It was her!" cried Grita.

"Shut that child up," yelled one of the justices. "Doesn't this child have a mother?"

The three justices and Oscar Vargas looked around for Doña Clara.

My sister now was really crying, and my mother—my mother just kept rocking in her chair.

"Who are you Romandías? What are you?" asked Oscar Vargas. "Not one of you has responded in a way commensurate with the severity of these proceedings."

"Hear, hear," yelled out one woman in the audience.

"I wish to simply point out," Oscar Vargas

continued, "the preposterousness of having a parrot speak for a family."

"Objection," said my father at this. "Soraida is eminently the most qualified and learned of all of us. Why she has . . . er . . . hmmn . . . studied . . . ah . . . abroad."

By now the big tree was spreading its shadow from one corner of the courtyard to the other. The plants in the coffee tins looked wilted as if they too were getting ready for bed.

It was now that Tío Jaime commenced his second set of Yoga exercises. He started to breathe loudly.

Abuelita said, "What a good boy."

Tío Rico said, "What a goody-two-shoes," shoving Tío Jaime aside. He ran to the bathroom as usual to primp for a night out with his friends.

It was getting close to dinner time and nothing had been set. Not a chicken had been plucked. Hortensia Salsipuedes must have forgotten.

"That is exactly what I mean," said Oscar

Vargas. "The parrot is the only one present with its wits about it. What is one to do?"

"Lights!" yelled one of the justices.

The two other justices took off their robes and placed them neatly in a pile, revealing unflattering short-sleeved shirts. The men removed their curly white wigs and piled them on the robes. Looking now just like any of the spectators, the two scooted off to the corner where they hauled out large round frog-like contraptions that turned out to be spot lights.

Some of the vendors that had been doing business just outside our courtyard door began setting up large grills and putting chopped wood in their wells, igniting the kindling to grill eucalyptus steaks or sear flattened chicken breasts.

Waiters from the cantina across the street came in and set up small tables with white cloths, taking care to place colored lanterns on each of the tables.

"Death," intoned the Chief Justice. "The sentence is death."

CHAPTER EIGHTEEN

s it the fever that does not let me forget? Not for a moment, not for a breath? It is so hot. So hot all I can do is sleep and dream. Dream about the bright waters and the washed skies and the trees that weep into their own branches.

Where does a memory come from? Did it slip in one night while I slept? Some early morning before I was quite awake? Or was it in the bright blankness of afternoon, when the air was still and my bones like metal—was that when it happened?

"Death," said Oscar Vargas. "Death," he repeated.

"This is insufferable!" yelled Soraida. "Unconscionable." She flew up to the banister overlooking the courtyard. "You barge into our courtyard," she railed at the Magistrate and the justices, "abuse our hospitality, order us to entertain you with our lifetime repertoire of stories and then you have the nerve to pronounce a sentence of death upon our house?"

"Well, yes," responded Oscar Vargas. "It is a very satisfactory ending to what has been a very long day."

The Chief Justice stood up. "Hear, hear, Magistrate Vargas, we heartily concur. Will you please read the findings of this court?"

"With pleasure," replied Oscar Vargas, accepting from the justice a long scroll of parchment.

I could tell that Soraida was flustered. She was flying from one end of the courtyard to the other, flapping her wings, letting out a frightful screak.

"But they are all innocent," she wailed. "Innocent as babes."

"No one is innocent," said Oscar Vargas, "when they have incited *you* to treason!"

"Yes!" yelled out one of the many assembled citizens of Aguas Calientes. "Treason!"

"Doing not a thing with their lives," Oscar Vargas blurted on. "You have only to look at their hands!"

I watched my father look at his fingernails recently buffed pink. I saw Abuelita look down at *her* hands. Tío Jaime looked at the finger holding his place in his chess manual. Tío Rico was in the bathroom down the hall and God only knows what *he* was looking at.

"Not an honest day's work has ever been done by any of those hands," insisted Oscar Vargas.

"So?" asked Soraida. "The Romandías do not have to work. That is not their talent."

"But that *is* their problem," said Oscar Vargas. "They have too much time on their hands— to invent seditious prattle for the likes of you."

"The Romandías are not only innocent, they are *innocents*," argued Soraida. "Wayward romantics, certainly. Feckless, yes, and, all right, hapless, but they are dreamers. And dreamers must be cherished—for they have the wisdom of the world. It is only the dreamers who have the secret of life."

We heard a deep clang, and then a voice.

"Hear ye, hear ye," intoned Oscar Vargas, "the Traveling Circuit Court will now make known its findings of fact and conclusions of law."

The audience applauded. That bunch of nobodies was becoming more and more insufferable, what with their loud eating and running commentaries.

"Find what?" asked Soraida. "Based on what? My recitations?"

"On facts, that's what," said Oscar Vargas. "First: The Romandía family, to wit: dusty grandmother, witless parents, spineless girls and oddball uncles—misfits and strange ducks to a one—is found wanting."

"Objection!" shrieked Soraida. "Objection, that is not a finding of anything. The Romandías are sitting ducks."

"As to the accused retainer," went on Oscar Vargas, "one maid answering to the name of Hortensia Salsipuedes, we the Traveling Circuit Court find her guilty as sin of *Santerías*, *brujerías*,

178

Devil worship, unrequited lust and the baking of greasy and heavy *arepas*, which alone justifies the sentence of death, the crueler and more unusual the better."

There was whistling and laughing in the courtyard, a collective slapping of thighs.

Oscar Vargas went on. "The accused defendant Soraida, Parrot, we find to be merely the dupe and agent of the despicable Romandía family."

"Objection!" Soraida shouted out once more. "I am nobody's dupe and agent. I am divine!"

It was best when Soraida was incensed to get out of her way, but I imagined Oscar Vargas could not have known that, and I am sure that he could have cared less.

So, too, she must have been hungry, at least as hungry as I was, for I knew that Soraida liked her victuals punctually, and it was really getting to be way past dinner.

Some of the audience was beginning to line up, plates in hand, at the vendors' grills. I overheard Oscar Vargas complain to one of the justices that he was suffering from heart burn—it must have been all those black beans he had had at lunch.

"Hear ye, hear ye," he resumed. "The Traveling Circuit Court finds the Romandía family— Guilty—guilty as charged of all the sins and omissions of which they have been accused. What have you to say for yourselves?"

"Err . . . ah . . . hmmm," said my father. "This is simply not possible."

"Don't worry, it will happen to all of us," said Oscar Vargas. "Some time or another."

CHAPTER NINETEEN

I am not sure what it is that makes some people think that they can get away with saying anything or doing anything, while other people have to sit there and take it and say not a single word in protest. I do know that Oscar Vargas was vile to all of us, and that we just sat there and took it.

"Sooner or later," he said to my father, "we all must go—poof. It is now your misfortune that this reality will come sooner rather than later."

My heart stopped—I tried to speak, but all I could say was "Feathers!" I saw feathers upon feathers, green ones mostly but some red, blue, and yellow, too—billows of them. Soraida's feathers! There was so much wind, so much dust biting into my face.

Oscar Vargas reached for the cold cigar sitting in the wide metal ashtray with the word CINZANO printed diagonally across it and struck a match with the tip of his longish thumbnail. He relit the cigar, exhaling a repugnant vapor of breath. (I was reminded of Soraida's observation that men sport cigars because their peckers are small—not for nothing, then, had she addressed him as "peanut dick.")

"In my line of work, one naturally sees criminals, drunks, vagrants of all sorts, cranks who are convinced that Martians are landing tomorrow at half-past noon because the transistors in their teeth have told them so. But this, *this*," he raised his voice, "this group of crazies takes the cake. *Coño*.

"And as for you," said Oscar Vargas, turning again on Soraida, "you wattled colostomy bag, you are full of nothing but parrot palaver."

At this, the Chief Justice turned to Oscar Vargas and said, "There is no need for personal invective, however apt. The facts here more than speak for themselves. Proceed, please."

Unfazed, Oscar Vargas went on. "We the Traveling Circuit Court therefore find the above mentioned Romandía family pointless and therefore superfluous and we recommend that the death be slow and excruciating and, if all goes well, humiliating to each and every one of them."

He sat down and wiped at his neck.

The air which had been still began to stir. I felt a breeze tickle my shins. My chest felt as if two hands had taken hold of my heart and squeezed it.

My father shrugged his shoulders and turned to Soraida as if to ask, "Now what are we going to do?"

Tío Jaime with an open palm gesture raised his slumped shoulders and said, "Epa, epa," meaning nothing at all.

Tío Rico sucked his lips into a grimace, flattening his nose with one finger and pulling his eyelids downwards with two others to show red.

My Abuelita opened her eyes wide, and her chicken-feather eyelashes reached all the way up to her brows.

"I do not want to die," cried Grita piteously, grabbing at her own neck. "Will it hurt?"

My mother rocked in her chair.

"This is impossible," said Soraida. "We will appeal!"

"There is no time for such niceties," said Oscar Vargas. "And you should know that time is of the essence."

"When is the sentence scheduled to be carried out?"

"As soon as possible. We are very tired."

"How is the sentence to be executed?"

"The old way. You know."

"No," said Soraida.

"*Sí*," said Oscar Vargas. "*Sí.*"

The sky was getting darker and darker. It was quite possibly past our bedtime.

"Wait!" shouted Soraida.

My mother was whistling softly to herself: what sounded like one of Tío Rico's tangos. The night creatures started to make their evening sounds.

"*Qué pasa?*" said Oscar Vargas.

"There must be a way out of this madness."

"It is too late. The sentence is as unappealable as it is so very appealing, such a pity."

"This is positively insane. You can't kill innocent people just like that."

"Yes, we can," said Oscar Vargas, stepping on a large waterbug as if to make his point. "We do it all the time."

"Look here, my man," said Soraida. "I have jewels. A ransom of them."

"What kind of jewels?" asked the Magistrate.

"Oh, so many kinds," trilled Soraida. "So many admirers over so much time."

"Hard to resell," said Oscar Vargas. "On the secondary market they can never fetch their true worth."

"I know there's a way. There's always a way. Let me see that." Soraida lunged at one of the justices who until now had been leafing through a thick tome in front of his eyes. Before the man realized what had happened, Soraida sat down on the book. The justice leapt up as if a spider had fallen on him and tried to shake Soraida off his book. Soraida clung.

"Give me that," said the justice.

"Not on your life, you old fart! Let go of that book. This is our lives!"

But the man held on. Soraida had no recourse but to bite him. "Ouwww," yelled the justice, clutching his hand.

Soraida grabbed the book and flew with it to the balustrade, using her long fore nail to flip through the pages, scanning them with those speedy eyes of hers much faster and more urgently than the justice had done.

"Aha," she exclaimed. "Here it is! I knew it!"

She flew down carrying the book to where the sullen justice was sucking on his finger, bobbing his head up and down.

"Look at this!"

"Why should I?"

"Because you're supposed to be a gentleman of the law."

"Hehmpf," the justice looked at the book.

Finally he admitted, "There does seem to be an exception."

"Well," said Soraida. "Read it aloud. Go on."

The justice took his finger out of his mouth long enough to point it. "Right here it says in Section 9343 of the Special Code of the Ultimate Statutes of the Republic dealing with *vagos* and *malientes*, parentheses in cases of capital punishment if and when applicable a parrot that has been taught to speak may and indeed should be sacrificed in lieu of any human victim. End of parentheses."

"Oh, no," yelled Grita. "Soraida!"

"It can't be," I cried out, too. Not my darling, not my friend.

But Soraida seemed pleased with her imminent martyrdom.

"String up the featherous foul mouth," yelled someone.

"Shoot dead the numinous windbag," shouted another.

"The matter is already settled. We are going to kill the lot of them. Useless malingerers. Right now," said Oscar Vargas. "*Ahora.* It is too late."

"But you can't," cried Soraida. "You mustn't."

"Bye, bye, Birdie!"

"But the law says there is an exemption, an exemption . . ."

"I refuse to even entertain the thought," said Oscar Vargas. "My job is done—I will have rid the world of the Romandías."

Soraida paused and inhaled as deeply as she could. "Take *me,* not them."

"And miss out on the continued pleasure of your company? That would be too cruel," said Oscar Vargas.

"I would never give you the pleasure of my company," said Soraida. "Listen," she now turned to the spectators. "You all heard it, the exception. The Romandías must not be made to die at the whim of this heartless Magistrate. If there is no law for them, then what kind of law will there be for you when your time comes—and it will, it will."

The audience jeered. "Down with dictators! Down with Magistrates!"

"Oh, all right, I am hungry—let the parrot do whatever she wants before she incites this rabble to riot." This last remark was whispered to the Chief Justice.

At this, Soraida stretched her wings out to their fullest. A thunderous noise rent the air; a vein of light split the sky; the wind heaved as if gasping for breath. Dust blew in our faces, feathers flew here and everywhere—chicken feathers, parrot feathers.

Grita began crying for Soraida. I heard footsteps running first one way, then another—the sound of *alpargatas* slapping on tile.

Nothing was visible. Nothing was clear.

Things change so quickly in a tropical clime.

One minute the sun is out and the streets are shining and then it darkens and blackens and the rains come down.

When the wind funneled back to the jungles and the dust settled and the waters dried up, then and only then could I see, in the center of that now famous yard, that topsy-turvy court-yard where the tiles were all aswirl, where people were sentenced to die or—sometimes worse—go on living, there in the dead-center, one foot in the drain hole and one tattered wing stretched out, was Soraida.

A drop of blood clung to the tip of her beak. She seemed to be asleep.

She was murmuring something, barely audible, half-words, snatches of a tune perhaps. *Adiós muchachos*, I thought she whispered. "So-long companions," I thought she sighed.

And before we could scream, "Stop, stop, oh, please God stop and take pity!" a woman from among the spectators had broken through and was reaching out for Soraida. And more women followed, for feather by feather they plucked Soraida until she looked more like a chicken than a glorious parrot, and then, as if she *were*—or had been—a mere chicken—they put her in a pot.

A simmering soup pot.

Coming to a boil.

It must have been the heat, the heat that made good things go bad, turn sour soft and venomous. It made all things go this way and that. Everything was sliding and slithering about.

It was just too hot. Too hot for thinking. Too hot for singing the words to a tango I once knew but forgot.

All I can do is sleep.

And dream.

It must be the fever that does not relent that does not let me for a moment forget.

Life is but a breath.